FAMOUS REGIMENTS

The Welsh Guards

FAMOUS REGIMENTS

The Welsh Guards

by John Retallack

with a Foreword by
HRH The Prince of Wales,
Colonel, Welsh Guards

FREDERICK WARNE

Published in Great Britain by
Frederick Warne (Publishers) Ltd, 1981
© *John Retallack 1981*

FOR DAVID BRUCE
Most loyal of Welsh Guardsmen
who started this book

ISBN 0 7232 2746 2

Printed in Great Britain by
Ebenezer Baylis & Son Limited
The Trinity Press, Worcester, and London
1460 · 680

CONTENTS

Contents

BUCKINGHAM PALACE

Our regimental histories of both world wars are now out of print, and there is a need not only to bring them together in wieldy form, but to bring the story of the Welsh Guards up to the present time.

Much has happened since 1945 and nothing reflects the change in the state of world affairs more vividly than the variety which to-day's 'peace-time' soldiering offers to the modern Guardsman compared to his father who served in the nineteen twenties and thirties. On training or on active service, the Regiment has done duty in the heat of the Radfan, in the Arctic Circle and from Texas to Chelsea Barracks.

In such a short book it is impossible to mention by name all those whose deeds have contributed to the high reputation of the Welsh Guards. But all good regiments are a team, and in a very real sense a family which extends beyond its battalions. I hope that this book will be of interest, not only to Welsh Guardsmen past and present, but to that wider family of parents, wives and all Welshmen who are proud of their Regiment of Foot Guards.

LIST OF PLATES

(following page 84)

PROLOGUE

Wales has always been known for the patriotism and the fighting qualities of her people. Although defeated by the Romans at the battle of Anglesea in AD 61, their conquerors continued to treat them with respect and were compelled to keep a legion at Chester for the next 400 years to guard the Welsh Marches. They never really penetrated the valleys, any more than the Saxons and then the Normans who followed them.

The last of the independent Welsh princes, Llewellyn ap Griffith, died in 1281. He had fought and lost against Edward I. But it had taken that great soldier several years of ruthless campaigning to bring the last pockets of resistance under control. In 1301 he created his son, later Edward II, Prince of Wales. The twentieth of these princes to be appointed, also an Edward, was the first Colonel of the Welsh Guards from 1919 to 1936. The Colonel today is his great-nephew, and is descended from Henry Tudor, the first King of England of truly Welsh blood.

Although the Welsh Guards are a comparatively new regiment, their badge has an old and honourable tradition. It is said that Cadwallawn's men had plucked leeks from a nearby field, as their distinguishing mark, before defeating the Saxons in a great battle in AD 633. Shakespeare, who had a feel for history, mentions it in *Henry V*. On the night before Agincourt, 1415, Fluellen says to the King: 'Welshmen did good service in a garden where leeks did grow . . . and I do believe your Majesty takes no scorn to wear the leek upon Saint Tavy's Day.' To which the King replies, 'I wear it for memorable honour; for I am Welsh, you know, good countryman.'

Welshmen have done much 'good service' to the Crown since the days of Edward I. But it was not until 27 September 1915, at the Battle of Loos, that the leek was once again proudly borne as the badge of the Welsh soldier.

1 FORMATION

The story of the Welsh Guards started, officially, on 26 February 1915, when a Royal Warrant, signed by King George V, authorized 'The formation of a Welsh Regiment of Foot Guards, to be designated the "Welsh Guards".'

Less officially the story had started on 6 February, when Field-Marshal Lord Kitchener, Secretary of State for War, sent for Major-General Sir Francis Lloyd, commanding the London District. There is surprisingly little formal record of the formation of the Welsh Guards, but General Lloyd made a note of this interview:

Lord Kitchener, very abruptly: 'You have got to raise a regiment of Welsh Guards.'
Sir Francis Lloyd: 'Sir, there are many difficulties in the way which I would like to point out first.'
Lord Kitchener, very rudely: 'If you do not like to do it, someone else will.'
Sir Francis Lloyd: 'Sir, when do you want them?'
Lord Kitchener: 'Immediately.'
Sir Francis Lloyd: 'Very well, Sir, they shall go on guard on St David's Day.'

Of the three old regiments of Foot Guards—Grenadiers, Coldstream and Scots—only the Scots Guards had a national affiliation. But with the formation of the Irish Guards in 1900, the claim of Wales for a similar distinction became obvious, and began to be pressed. But the times were not

1

ripe for any expansion of the army; however the outbreak of war in 1914 offered the opportunity.

Whether or not the inspiration was entirely Lord Kitchener's, he certainly gave the push. But in fulfilling the aspirations of the Welsh people, he may have had further reasons. Kitchener was a great admirer of the Brigade of Guards, their training, discipline and professionalism, and he may already have had at the back of his mind the formation of the Guards Division, which he brought into being, equally abruptly five months later (a curt letter to the Commander-in-Chief in France, another curt interview with General Lloyd).

On 27 February, the day after the signing of the Royal Warrant, the new regiment began assembling at the White City. Two days later they mounted guard on Buckingham Palace on St David's Day, as promised by Sir Francis Lloyd. This apparently miraculous speed is explained by the fact that the Commanding Officer, Lieutenant-Colonel W. Murray-Threipland, had been told by Kitchener to go ahead a few days before the announcement, without waiting for the official grindings of the War Office. Even so it was quick work; and on that first guard, officers and men still wore the badges of their previous regiments. The Captain of the Guard was the Commanding Officer himself.

Murray-Threipland proved to be an inspired choice to raise the new regiment. He was a Grenadier of great experience who had seen service in the Sudan and in the South African War. From the moment of his transfer, the Welsh Guards became the ruling passion of his life. Only the highest standards were acceptable; in return he gave his utmost. His second-in-command was Major The Hon. A. G. A. Hore-Ruthven, VC, later to become Regimental Lieutenant-Colonel, Colonel of the Regiment, and a distinguished Governor-General of Australia. He had staunch support from his adjutant, Captain G. C. D. Gordon, immaculate as any adjutant should be, and a team of first-class warrant officers, headed by R.S.M. Stevenson. Even so, the Commanding Officer had a difficult and delicate task.

In the first place, in any institution with a long and honourable history attended by much success, like the Brigade of Guards, there is always opposition to change, and it is not too much to say that the formation of the Welsh Guards had shocked a number of senior officers, both serving and retired. And if there was no active opposition, the performance of the new regiment would inevitably be regarded with a very critical eye. If they did well, it would be because they had had so many transfers from the old regiments; if they did not do well, then the critics would have been right in the first place. This was a difficulty which only time and success would overcome.

The second, and immediate, difficulty was the choice of officers, warrant officers and NCOs. In an established regiment officers and men are known and proved over a number of years. In this case they had to be taken on trust or very quickly judged. But the Commanding Officer's discrimination was sure and rapid, and in six months he forged a regiment that was to be worthy of both Wales and the Brigade of Guards.

There was much else to be done. On 19 March the King approved the colours and sanctioned the title of Prince of Wales Company for the leading company of the 1st Battalion. Details regarding uniform were also settled. The leek was chosen for the cap-badge, and the plume for the bearskin was to be white-green-white, the Tudor colours. Regimental marches were also chosen: 'The Rising of the Lark' for the quick march and 'Men of Harlech' for the slow.

Recruitment went well; both direct recruitment from Wales and, following an appeal from the Major-General, himself a Welshman, transfers from other regiments of the Brigade of Guards. There were also transfers from the Army as a whole; both these last two sources provided valuable experience to the new regiment.

Much hard training was carried out, first at the White City among the swings and roundabouts of the now deserted fun-fair, and then at Sandown Park, Esher. As the time for the Battalion's departure for France became nearer, a 2nd (Reserve) Battalion was formed to provide the 1st Battalion with trained reinforcements. It was also necessary to form a proper Regimental Headquarters. On the formation of the Regiment, Lieutenant-Colonel Murray-Threipland had doubled as Commanding Officer of the 1st Battalion and as Regimental Lieutenant-Colonel. On 16 June 1915 the latter appointment was taken over by Lord Harlech.

Their arrangements thus made, the new Regiment lay waiting and ready for whatever fate might bring them in war. For a short spell they carried out public duties in London, but two events were still needed to give recognition to their efforts so far. On 3 August they received their Colours from the King at a parade in the gardens of Buckingham Palace, and on 7 August the King became their Colonel-in-Chief. These were great but still formal honours; the real accolade they could only earn for themselves in battle.

Early on 17 August the 1st Battalion, Welsh Guards, left Waterloo Station for Southampton on their way to join the Guards Division in France.

Just over a year previously, during the long, hot summer of 1914, the smouldering rivalries of the great European powers had burst into flame. On 28 June the Archduke Franz Ferdinand, heir to the throne of Austria, was assassinated on an official visit to Sarajevo, capital of the Austrian province of Bosnia. There followed a quick fuse of uncontrolled events. Austria accused Serbia of complicity in the assassination. As fellow Slavs, the Serbs were supported by Russia. Germany gave guarantees to Austria; the French had obligations to Russia, and the British to the French. Unwilling to be caught at a disadvantage, the governments of these powerful countries set in motion the implacable juggernaut of mobilization. Last-minute attempts at peace were of no avail; the military machine had taken over.

The immediate spark for Great Britain was Germany's disregard for the neutrality of Belgium, which they invaded in a great sweep to outflank the French defences along the Franco–German border. Occupation of the Channel Ports by Germany would have given her powerful navy bases far too close to the English shores for comfort. Almost willy-nilly, Great Britain declared war on Germany on 4 August.

After the first few weeks, during which the Germans made a dash for Paris and a quick victory, The Great War, particularly in France, became a war of position. After the German advance was halted, both sides dug in, and by the autumn their two lines of trenches stretched from Switzerland to the English Channel. The ground between them was dominated by artillery, the machine gun and barbed wire. Great battles, with appalling casualties, were fought for possession of a few miles of territory. Both sides were supported by an enormous number of guns, which were seldom silent. Attacks were preceded by lengthy bombardment, which not only forfeited any chance of surprise, but reduced the battle zone to a swathe of desolation across France. Towns, villages and hamlets became little more than names on a map, remembered on the ground by nothing more than a heap of rubble and a roughly painted sign.

Because of the incessant shellfire, the land-drainage system was destroyed, and from early autumn to late spring an unimaginable mud made the movement of men and supplies a slow, and at times an almost impossible, business. Men and even horses could, and often did, drown in the mud.

For nearly four years neither side was able to break the lethal deadlock, and it was against this background, and these conditions, that the Welsh Guards first saw action at the Battle of Loos.

2 THE GREAT WAR:
A BITTER STRUGGLE

Loos—1915

On 20 August the 1st Battalion joined the Guards Division, which was forming near St Omer, as part of 3rd Guards Brigade. The Division, with the rest of 1st British Army, was training for the first of the tremendous set-piece battles of the Great War, which was to become known as the Battle of Loos.

After nearly a year of static, trench-bound, operations, the British and French were planning a large-scale attempt to break through the German lines and restore open warfare. The country favoured the defence. It was either open and without cover, or dotted with an intricate maze of mines, slag heaps and villages. Loos itself was a mining town, with behind it a large, bare hill known as Hill 70. The Guards Division was in reserve, ready to exploit the expected breakthrough.

The leading divisions attacked at 6.30 a.m. on 25 September, with varying success. On the right Loos was cleared, but not Hill 70 which overlooked it. Similar patchy results were obtained elsewhere on a front of about five miles. There was a fleet moment when the coveted breakthrough almost occurred. But the reserves were too far back, and when the attack was continued on the 26th it had lost any real bite; the Germans had had time to recover; they even regained some lost ground.

6

During the opening stages of the battle, the Guards Division was making an arduous approach march along choked roads, sometimes in pouring rain. By the evening of the 26th they were committed, not to a breakthrough, but to holding what had been gained. 1st and 2nd Guards Brigades went on to relieve the two leading divisions in the line; 3rd Guards Brigade remained in reserve in the village of Vermelles, three miles short of Loos.

The Battalion arrived there in the morning to find the place awash with the overflow of battle: guns blazing, men and transport moving up, and the tired columns of wounded making their way back. At 2.30 p.m. they got the order to move on to Loos, concentrate there, and with 4th Grenadiers capture Hill 70 that night.

The approach to Loos was the Welsh Guards' first experience of war. From Vermelles the ground rises gently for about a mile followed by an easy slope down to Loos itself. As soon as they came over the crest they were seen by the enemy who opened heavy shellfire as they crossed the skyline. Shrapnel burst in puffs overhead and high explosive threw up pillars of mud and black smoke. Both Grenadiers and Welshmen went steadily forward, down into Loos, which reeked with gas.[1] The Battalion found shelter in an abandoned German trench on the edge of the village, while the Commanding Officer went on into Loos to get orders from the Brigadier. He presently returned and led the Battalion through the village to the further outskirts where they found what protection they could. The gas shelling was now so bad that they had to put on the stifling bags which then did service as gas-masks.

Late in the afternoon the Commanding Officer gave orders for the Battalion to attack Hill 70. It was about 6 p.m. and the light was already failing when the attack started. At first there was a guide-mark of a clump of trees on the skyline,

[1] The Germans first used gas on the Western Front against the French at Ypres on 22 April 1915.

but this faded as night fell. The companies groped their way forward in the dark but somehow managed to keep direction.

They knew at once when they reached the top of the hill. A star-shell went up, followed by another and another until they found themselves caught in a blaze of light, in which everything could be seen clearly. There was a scatter of rifle fire and then a crash of well-directed machine gun fire, so intense that it was described as having the force of some natural phenomenon such as a typhoon. But such intensity cannot last, and when it died down a little, men were able to dig themselves small scrapes or roll into shell-holes. Somehow companies found touch with each other and managed to establish a line just below the crest of the hill.

The question now was whether they could stay there. Enemy fire was still too heavy to allow the digging and wiring needed to establish a secure line. The Battalion had also been weakened by casualties. The Commanding Officer therefore judged and recommended to the Brigade Commander that he should be relieved by 2nd Scots Guards. This was agreed, and after a reconnaissance by both Commanding Officers it was decided that to dig an integrated line of defence on the crest would be impossible. But an old German trench was discovered about 100 yards below the top of the hill. This was strengthened, wired and occupied by the Scots Guards, while the Welsh still clung to the crest of the hill.

The Welsh Guards then had the difficult task of withdrawing, under fire, with their wounded. They achieved this by daybreak on the 28th, when they reformed in Loos, where they remained in close support until the following day, when they marched back to Vermelles.

The Battle of Loos continued to rage. After a few days' rest the Guards Division was re-engaged, this time on the left flank of the attack, where the critical point was the Hohenzollern Redoubt. This was a maze of trenches, wire and fortifications which had been the keystone of the

German defences, and which had been captured in the initial attack on 25 September.

During the following month the Battalion spent four periods in the line alternating with three or four days in billets and one period in the redoubt itself. But they were not actively engaged except for taking part in a number of bombing raids, either on their own account, or in support of other battalions in the Division. It was here, where the lines were very close to each other, that the Battalion was hailed in Welsh from the opposing lines. It turned out that before the war the speaker had been a barber in Cardiff and had even cut the hair of some of them.

There was a steady drain of casualties, it was wet, and the trenches stank abominably. The Germans had not hesitated to use their dead to build up their defences, and here and there a parapet or trench wall thrust out a clammy and derisive hand. At night the chalky soil, ravaged of vegetation by high explosive, shimmered white under the moon.

By 27 October the Guards Division was finally withdrawn. The Welsh Guards marched to billets at Allouagne. Neither place nor name would be memorable, except that it was here that the new regiment found its lasting spirit and personality, the indefinable but positive character that any good regiment has. It might be supposed that this would have been forged in the fighting at Loos, but that would only be half the story. Under the spur of action, good men tend to do well, even to surpass themselves. But the reaction following the sudden release from the strains of battle brings its own more insidious strains. There is a feeling of lassitude, small jobs are skimped, turnout falls off, nothing seems worth while. Experienced battalions know this and know how to deal with it. The Welsh Guards, only eight months and one battle old, but with already 171 casualties after their formation, were not ready for it. They had acquitted themselves well in action; they now had to battle with themselves. Good sense, discipline, training and familiar routine prevailed. Doubly tried and proved, the Battalion assured not only their own future, but that of their successors.

Winter 1915–16—the Ypres Salient

The fighting at Loos, and later at other great battles such as the Somme or Passchendaele, was long and bitter; but fighting of such violence cannot last. There were longer periods, during which a pattern was evolved, when the troops followed a routine of rest, reserve and front-line duty. Periods which the newspapers at home reported as quiet, a description which the soldiers read with wry amusement. It was just such a routine which the Battalion followed during the months after Allouagne. The pattern varied according to the requirements of the different sectors of the front. A fairly typical routine was established in the Ypres Salient, which the Guards Division garrisoned from March to July 1916.

In the Salient a battalion could expect to spend six days in the front line, six in brigade reserve in billets, and six days further back in divisional reserve. There were, in addition, periods when they were removed from the front altogether to rest areas.

Billets varied; in forward areas, reasonable billets would be farm buildings with plenty of dry straw which allowed a man to make himself comfortable with his blankets and a groundsheet. They could be worse—in wet, half-ruined cottages. In proper rest areas they could be better—a hutted camp with facilities for baths, cinemas, concert parties and football fields. But even in the best of billets the war was never far away and the guns rumbled on.

The aim of rest periods was not merely the negative one of release from the strain and effort of the front line; a positive programme had to be followed. First there was the question of health. It might be supposed that the hard, open life of the trenches would breed hard, fit men. The opposite was the case; poor food, filthy conditions and nervous strain had a weakening effect. For example after one long, five-week spell in the trenches or close reserve, when the Battalion marched back to billets, only some 14 miles, 23 men fell out and collapsed unconscious. As a first priority in a rest area men had to be well fed, exercised and provided with proper baths. Feet had to be cared for, socks darned, boots repaired, clothing, equipment and weapons maintained. All the small exchange of good administration, and therefore good morale, had to be meticulously accounted for.

The second requirement was training. Again it might be supposed that a thoroughly battle-hardened battalion is a well-trained battalion. Again the reverse is the case; battle-hardened soldiers are also battle weary. They become careless, unnecessary risks are taken and avoidable casualties mount up. Also, during a long war, new techniques, weapons and equipment are developed and must be learned. During rest periods the opportunity was therefore taken to send officers and men on courses of instruction.

But there was play as well as work. The Guards Division had its own cinema; there were concert parties, football matches and even race meetings. Reading rooms were established and good canteens. And quite near the front, imperturbable French patrons would keep their restaurants and cafés open, just as the dour French farmer continued to till his fields within a mile or two of the lines, well within range of the guns.

In close reserve, although perhaps in reasonable billets, life was exhausting and often dangerous. Battalions in brigade reserve, as well as having to be ready for immediate action, were burdened with all the heavy fatigues needed to keep the system going. Above all this meant digging—the endless business of keeping in good repair trenches which collapsed under the next bout of heavy shellfire, or parapets which were washed away by the next downpour of rain. There were stores and ammunition to be humped up to the front line, awkward and heavy loads to be negotiated along narrow, winding trenches, often under fire and with a steady drain of casualties.

The line itself was a system usually composed of a forward trench with two further trenches supporting it, and with communicating trenches running between, the whole locked together by strongpoints with machine guns. Running forward from the front trench were saps, or small trenches, leading to advanced listening posts. In front again was the endless barbed wire. Men lived in dug-outs burrowed into the trench walls, with enough overhead cover to withstand a direct hit from anything but a heavy shell.

This all sounds neater and tidier than in fact it was. In the ebb and flow of battle, the text-book layout became a maze of disused trenches that led nowhere, back to where you started from, or even, occasionally, into the trenches of your opponents.

The basic routine of trench life at the time is indicated by a battalion order:

All work will be done during the hours of darkness. There will be no moving about by day. Teas and rifle inspection will be carried out just before dark, work from dark to midnight—dinners at midnight—work to recommence at 1 a.m. until 'stand to arms', which will be for not less than twenty minutes. Teas and inspection of arms, after which every one will dismiss until evening.

Patrols went out each night into 'no-man's-land', crawling and slithering in and out of the shell-holes to gain information about the enemy's positions, routine and movements, and at the same time to deny him the opportunity of gaining the same information about the British.

Raids had the object of harassing the enemy, taking prisoners to identify opposing units, or improving the layout of a battalion's position. These raids varied in size from a dozen or so men to elaborate forays involving a whole battalion, with strong artillery support. A typical example was the raid at Mortaldje, in this case to improve the

Battalion's position, by No 4 Company under Captain Insole.

The objective was the Mortaldje estaminet, or the remains of it: a heap of rubble and a couple of girders. Incorporated into the German lines, garrisoned with two troublesome machine guns, it had become a running sore, jutting forward to within 70 yards of the British trenches. The aim of the raiding party was to reverse the situation.

The operation, rehearsed down to the last detail, took place on the night of 1 July 1916, supported by a heavy artillery bombardment. At first all went well, the estaminet was taken without casualties and a number of prisoners captured. But time and conditions were against the raiding party: the summer night was short, and even in summer the ground was waterlogged. As fast as they dug new positions, they filled with water, or were blown in by German mortars. They also had to fight off a counter-attack. The small battle[1] continued until 11 p.m. the following evening, when the party withdrew. Although they had been unable to maintain themselves in the estaminet, they established two bombing posts which denied it to the enemy.

The Somme 1916:
Ginchy—Flers-Courcelette—Morval

On the same day that No 4 Company were engaged in their raid on Mortaldje, away to the south the armies of Great Britain and France launched their greatest attempt yet to break through the German lines. The ground on the Somme front entirely favoured the German defence. The British positions were on a flat, unrelieved plain, and the Germans, who held the high ground, had complete observation of

[1] There is always a battle for someone on a 'quiet' sector of the front. This raid cost the Battalion 96 casualties. Similar raids during that week cost the Guards Division 261.

British preparation, movement and the advance itself. The British had always to attack up hill. This they did in long straight lines, almost shoulder to shoulder, their rifles held at an exact angle in front of them, and at a slow steady walk. For all that they were supported by 1,537 guns, or one to every 20 yards of front, these were the tactics of the eighteenth century.

Against the German machine guns, the infantry suffered accordingly. The attack, which started in glorious summer weather, with flocks of larks singing so brilliantly that they could be heard through the bellow of the guns, petered out in a shambles of 60,000 casualties in the first few hours. The sky that night, and for the next two nights, was a peculiarly deep red.

Ginchy

On 27 July the Battalion had left the Ypres Salient, and with the Guards Division moved by stages to the Somme area. By this time the Battle of the Somme had loosened up and more flexible tactics had emerged. The pitiless hail of lead from the German machine guns had imposed its own solution. The survivors of those first long, straight lines had broken up into small groups who, dodging from shell-hole to shell-hole, cover to cover, had stalked their tormentors, put them out of action and made some quite deep advances without further great loss.

Ginchy is a small hamlet surrounded by an irregularly shaped wood about 500 × 600 yards. Standing on high ground it stubbornly resisted any further British advance, so far some two and a half miles after six weeks' fierce fighting. It was part of the objective planned for an attack by 16th Division on 9 September. The Welsh Guards were to take over once it had been captured.

The attack on Ginchy itself was successful, but those on either side of it did not make the progress expected. Nevertheless that afternoon it was decided that, after dark, the

Battalion should relieve the attacking troops, who had been weakened by casualties. The plan was for Prince of Wales Company to cover the northeast corner of the wood, with 2 and 3 Companies on their left who would link up with another division. 4th Battalion Grenadier Guards were to come up on Prince of Wales Company's right.

The night was pitch dark, and as the Battalion moved forward it became apparent that Ginchy was not firmly in British hands. On the approach to it they came under scattered rifle fire and there were also small parties of Germans scuttling about among the ruined houses, though most of them surrendered without trouble.

Eventually, at about 3.30 a.m., the companies reported to Battalion Headquarters that they were in position. But in the dark they had veered away to their left, so that Prince of Wales Company faced northwest instead of northeast. The result was that although their left flank was secure on 2 and 3 Companies, their right flank was in the air.

A misty dawn brought with it a strong counter-attack, directed at their exposed flank, which swept into the wood, where some fierce hand-to-hand fighting took place. But the attack died away under the fire of Nos 2 and 3 Companies, who were able to fire across Prince of Wales Company's front. The wood itself was a tangled mass of broken trees, a few upright stumps, rubble from the houses and half destroyed German dug-outs. But so confused was the fighting that a man crouching for cover in one shell-hole did not know if the neighbouring shell-hole contained friend or foe.

At noon the Germans attacked again, and fighting was continuous for the rest of the day, often hand to hand, swaying back and forth through the wood and round the edges of it. By the end of the day the desperate attempts of the Germans to regain Ginchy petered out; attacks by their infantry ceased and their artillery switched to other targets. During the night the Welsh Guards, with the elements of

Grenadiers and Scotsmen to help them, managed to organize some sort of line, and many of the Germans still hidden in the wood gave themselves up. The following day, the 11th, was a quiet one; more prisoners were winkled out of dug-outs and shell-holes, and that evening the Battalion was relieved by the Grenadiers and Scots Guards.

It was a much thinned battalion that marched back to billets, where reinforcements waited to replace the 205 casualties they had suffered. Five days later they were in action again.

Flers-Courcelette

The capture of Ginchy provided a jumping-off place for the next phase of the advance, and on 14 September the Battalion moved back to a concentration area just behind the forward troops. It was here, at Trones Wood, that they had their first sight of the new tank, ten of which had been allotted to support the Guards Division in their big attack on the following day. The clattering, ungainly monsters caused the troops the only amusement they were to have for some days.

The attack by the Guards Division was part of a general attack by 4th British Army. There were three successive objectives until they reached the line of Fler, Morval, and then Les Boeufs. Each objective was about 1,200 yards behind the other, about two miles all told.

At 6.30 a.m., 1st and 2nd Guards Brigade debouched from the wood round Ginchy. This in itself was a movement of some difficulty. The capture of Ginchy had indeed provided a spring-board for further advance, but it was too restricted for the frontage of two brigades. The enemy still had a tight grip on both flanks; and as the attacking troops fanned out from the bottle-neck, they came under a winnowing fire from the Germans, who throughout this battle fought with notable skill and gallantry. And on this occasion with great effect. The attacks on either flank of the Guards were held up. The tanks, which were to have given support, did not arrive, and 1st and 2nd Guards Brigades, although they reached their first objective, were too disorganized and had too many casualties to go further.

At 1 a.m. on the 16th the Battalion received orders to continue the attack. The rain fell in sheets, communications were appalling, the orders, when they came, were a pulp of wet paper. Eventually the attack, with 4th Battalion Grenadiers on the right, started at midday, several hours late. Surprise had been lost and the result was a repetition of the day before. Some progress was made; in short, alternate section rushes they got as far as the Fler–Les Boeufs road. There they had to dig in some 200 yards short of their objective. It was a long day of hard, confused and continuous fighting, and not a little muddle. It was also a costly day; the price for less than 1,000 yards of flat, broken and featureless country was 144 killed and wounded.

That night they were relieved by 20th Division to get what rest they could—it was to be little enough. On 22 September they were back in the line, and on the 25th the attack continued.

Morval

When the Battalion went back into the line, they relieved the 4th Battalion Grenadier and the 2nd Battalion Scots Guards, who were due to lead 3rd Guards Brigade attack three days later. The objective was still that of 15/16 September, which, in spite of the great efforts of those two days, remained in enemy hands—a line running north of the villages of Les Boeufs[1] and Morval.

The Battalion was to be in reserve, with special responsibility for the left flank. As they waited in their reserve trenches, Battalion Headquarters were entertained by a

[1] Although the Guards Division was engaged against Les Boeufs, the official name of the battle, in which the whole of British 4th Army took part, was recorded as Morval.

maharajah, Major-General Sir Pertab Singh, in command of an Indian cavalry division. Impatient at the delay in launching his cavalry against the enemy, he repeatedly jumped his charger back and forth across the trench in his frustration at being held back.

Preceded by a bombardment which had started on the 23rd, on 25 September the attack went in, punctually, at 12.35 p.m. Now the troops moved forward behind a creeping barrage which rolled on at the rate of 50 yards a minute. On this occasion all went well, though not without hard fighting and casualties. Even the weather was kind and good progress was made over firm ground. Indeed it was this swift success that led to the sharpest fighting of the day.

By 3 p.m. the leading battalions were in possession of all their objectives. But while on the right they had advanced level with other attacking troops, on the left they had outrun them. In doing so they had left unattended an enemy strongpoint which immediately started to give trouble from a position that was now behind the Allied forward line.

Prince of Wales and 2 Companies were ordered to secure this open flank. By using every scrap of cover they managed to establish a firm line which covered Les Boeufs. Towards evening it was apparent that the Germans were beginning, at last, to lose heart. Small parties were seen trying to slip away; some were shot and others surrendered. That night was fairly quiet, and by dawn a good trench had been dug.

But the strongpoint still held out, and during the early hours of the morning, orders were received to capture it next day. The operation was never carried out. Soon after daybreak the Battalion, and the enemy, saw, for the first time, a tank go into action. Whether from mutual amazement, or for some other reason, a hush fell over the battlefield. In almost complete silence, except for a surprised shot or two, the new-fangled monster clanked, wheezed and lumbered towards the strongpoint. To a man the panic-stricken garrison of about 250 rushed out and surrendered, some to the tank, others to the delighted guardsmen. The troublesome flank was now safe.

That night the whole Division was relieved. Although casualties had been less than in the other Somme battles (the Welsh Guards had 78), the accumulation of casualties left them so under strength that they were sent to a rest area to re-fit and absorb reinforcements.

Winter 1916–17

By November the Battle of the Somme had died down, and the Battalion started on the routine of another long and bitter winter. The weather was, if possible, even more brutal than it had been the year before, and conditions were correspondingly worse. Billets were bad, trenches were sometimes non-existent. On occasion the front line was no more than a string of water-filled shell-holes about 20 yards apart. There were no communicating trenches; reliefs had to be carried out in the open, after long marches floundering through the mud. Conditions on the German side were as bad, or worse. In misery, both sides fought cold, wet, mud and snow rather than each other. Even patrolling had become impossible. The only activity, on either side, was provided by the artillery, which continued to churn and re-churn the mud; the infantry were stuck. Freedom of movement was available only to clouds of great bats, which could be seen as they flittered in the air over the trenches and no-man's-land on moonlit nights.

A small detail emphasizes the conditions. In December the newly formed Regimental Band was sent out to provide a little cheer over Christmas. They arrived as the Battalion was marching out of line; the men were so tired that they had to be played back to their billets in slow time.

It was in December, too, that the Commanding Officer was

forced to leave the Battalion owing to ill-health. More than any one man he had moulded the Regiment and the Battalion. All ranks sensed the kindliness under the somewhat dour exterior. And they responded to his demands for the highest standards because they knew that he placed their interests above his own. He had refused promotion to stay with them and was prepared to refuse an order if he considered it a waste of life. On one such occasion his adjutant, Captain J. A. D. Perrins, listened fascinated as he dug his toes in over the field telephone:

> . . . he absolutely refused. Brigade switched him through to Division, where I suppose he spoke to the Divisional Commander. . . . I can hear him now, repeating that the scheme[1] was crazy . . . was sheer murder . . . they could do what they liked with him, but he would never issue the order. I had never heard anyone speak to a superior officer like that before. . . . Anyway, the raid never did take place.

It is not surprising that the Battalion deeply felt the loss of such a man. Command of the Battalion was taken over by Lieutenant-Colonel Douglas Gordon, who had been adjutant right at the beginning.

At about this time changes in organization and weapons began to be introduced. When the Battalion first arrived in France, in common with the rest of the Infantry they were basically armed with rifle and bayonet only. There were four heavy machine guns, but these were taken away to become part of a centralized machine gun company under control of Brigade Headquarters. However, a new light machine gun, the Lewis gun, now began to be issued, first on a small scale and then in increasing numbers until there were 32 per battalion, the heavy machine guns remaining centralized. The Mills bomb became standard, and an effective trench mortar, the 'Stokes', was also issued.

---

[1] The scheme had been dreamed up by someone at Corps Headquarters. The idea was for a raid to be carried out in gas-masks; not because there was gas about, or because a raid was needed, but simply to see if it could be done.

The platoon now consisted of four sections, one of Lewis gunners, another of bombers, a third of rifle bombers, and a rifle section. Air power over the battlefield was also becoming a factor to be reckoned with, and each company had one Lewis gun detailed for anti-aircraft defence.

The first move of the campaigning season of 1917 was made by the Germans, when they shortened their line by withdrawing to a prepared position, known as the Hindenburg Line. The retreat was skilfully carried out; anything which might be of use to the British in their follow-up was destroyed: buildings blown up, roads blocked, bridges demolished and even wells filled in. This move had not been unexpected, and preparations had been made to snap as closely at the German heels as possible. Even so, the Germans managed to slip away without immediately being detected during the night of 13 March, and it was not until the following afternoon that the Guards Division noticed that they were gone. But by the following morning the German trenches had been occupied, and a cautious advance was carried out over the next few days. By the end of the month a new line had been established and the Guards Division was withdrawn for a well earned rest and training.

Early in 1917 two great events occurred which were to affect the course of the war. In Russia the Revolution broke out on 5 April, and on the 6th the United States of America entered the war against Germany. Neither event made any immediate impact on the fighting on the Western Front. The still moderate Russian government continued the war against Germany, and prevented her from switching troops from Russia to France. And the limitless resources of the Americans were not to be effectively brought to bear for another year.

What did affect the British was the unrest, and even mutiny, among the French troops. It was soon over, but the burden of the year's fighting was to fall heavily on the British armies.

Passchendaele 1917—Cambrai (Gouzeaucourt)

After the seemingly endless winter, the Guards Division was taken right out of the line, and the Battalion went to a rest area at Peronne. They were under canvas, but the weather smiled, and they were to be in one place long enough to settle down, relax, and with all the ingenuity of the British soldier, plus a little gentle looting, make themselves comfortable. Above all, the countryside round them was green and fresh. They even planted small gardens and held a gardening competition, though the brigadier who judged it was fairly sure that he spotted some of his own choice blooms smiling back at him from the winning plot. These two months were just the tonic that the Welsh Guards wanted, and it was a much refreshed, cheerful and vigorous battalion which made its way north to St Omer where they arrived on 31 May.

St Omer lay behind Ypres, the sector chosen for the next great autumn offensive by the Allies. This, the Third Battle of Ypres, more commonly came to be called Passchendaele, the name of the low, undistinguished ridge of ground which marked the end of the campaign, and where it drowned in a welter of mud, wasted heroism and wasted life.

The training for the coming attack was carried out in the greatest detail. The problem for the Guards Division lay in having to cross the muddy Yser Canal which ran between the British and German lines. Rehearsals took place on a training area, laid out to scale, which represented the ground over which the advance was to take place. The Battalion polished and repolished their role, clipping off a minute here and a few seconds there, until after six such rehearsals each man knew exactly what he was required to do. The day for the attack was finally fixed for 31 July; the preliminary bombardment started on the 22nd.

At the last moment there was a change of plan. 1st Guards Brigade had discovered that the German trenches were only lightly held, and on the 27th, without any warning bombardment, caught their opponents off-guard, slipped across the canal in broad daylight, and established a new front line about 500 yards beyond it. This meant that the Battalion could start their own attack with the advantage of having the Yser Canal behind them, and on the night of the 30th they moved across it to their assembly areas.

The attack was meticulously planned (the Battalion order runs to eleven closely-written pages), and follows exactly the formations laid down in the Infantry Manual of the time. Some detail is given here to illustrate a typical trench warfare attack in 1917.

The first assaulting wave was composed of, on the right, two platoons of No 2 Company and on the left, two platoons of No 3 Company. They were followed by two platoons of No 4 Company as 'moppers-up'. The other half of Nos 2 and 3 Companies made up the second wave; Prince of Wales Company complete made up the third wave, followed by the remainder of No 4 Company as their 'moppers-up'. The intervals between each wave was 60 yards, with the 'moppers-up' 15 yards behind the first and third waves. The distance between each man was about three yards. The objectives were: first wave, Blue Line; second and third waves, Black Line. The Grenadier and Scots Guards would then pass through and capture the final objective, Green Line. The total planned advance was about two and a half miles.

Punctually at 4.24 a.m. the barrage came down, 200 yards in front of the first wave, which immediately moved up to 50 yards behind it. The barrage then crept forward at 25 yards to the minute. No opposition was met with until the forward troops reached Wood 15, when they were held up on the right by machine guns in a concrete blockhouse which had been undamaged by the barrage which had now moved on. It was then that Sergeant Bye, having crawled to within striking distance, managed to rush the blockhouse from behind and bomb the occupants out of it. This allowed the first objective to be taken, and the second and third waves continued on to the next objective. Again the advance was held up, this time by another blockhouse away to the left in Wood 16. Again Sergeant Bye went forward, at a steady amble, tripping and falling on the uneven ground. Each time it seemed that he must have been killed, each time he got up and went on until, once more, he was behind the blockhouse which he successfully bombed. Once again the line was able to sweep forward to its objective. Sergeant Bye killed, wounded or captured over 70 men in these blockhouses, and for his truly inspired action that day he was awarded the Victoria Cross.

It was the first time that these blockhouses had been encountered. They proved to be quite elaborate affairs, containing up to four machine guns and with a complement of 50 men. And although they resisted damage from the creeping barrages which preceded the advancing troops, they were not invulnerable to determined, close-quarter attack, as Sergeant Bye had shown. Others quickly followed his example: Lieutenant R. R. Jones captured another by firing through a loophole, while his platoon dealt with the garrison as it tried to escape from the rear. Private 1209 Hughes led the way to yet another, also in Wood 16, which he out-flanked and captured.

By 8 a.m. the Battalion had captured both its objectives, and by 10 a.m. the Grenadiers had passed through and captured their objectives on the Green Line. Later in the day, other units of the Guards Division had advanced to the Steenbeck River, crossed it and consolidated a new line on the far side. The attack had gone like clockwork. By that evening, the Battalion had been relieved and were back in Elverdinghe.

The battle rumbled on until the end of October, but that first day was the last day of success: crisp, decisive actions with solid gains and comparatively light casualties. Other gains were made, but at increasing cost as the fighting once more floundered in the clutching mud and torrential rain. The story is exemplified by the casualty returns. On that first day the Battalion had 138 casualties; they were to hold the line on three more separate occasions, tours that were varied with periods of forward fatigues, training and rest. When they finally marched out, soaked to the skin, on 12 October, without having taken part in any gain to justify them, their casualties had mounted by another 313.

Cambrai (*Gouzeaucourt*)

A month after Passchendaele was called off, the British Army attacked again, at Cambrai, about 50 miles to the south. After their withdrawal from the Passchendaele front, the Battalion spent three weeks resting in billets near St Omer. They then moved by stages towards the Cambrai front. Cambrai is famous as the battle in which tanks were used in large numbers for the first time. The battle was a mixture of brilliant tactical success on the first day, and strategic failure.

The secret of the coming battle had been well kept. The attack started without any preliminary bombardment, and 318 tanks, supported by infantry, made advances of up to five miles (the equivalent of months of fighting on the Somme or at Passchendaele). The enemy's three defence lines were overrun and for the whole of that afternoon and evening their front lay wide open. Surprise had been complete. But the chance was not taken; the British seem to have been as surprised as the Germans by their success. Reserves were too far away, or did not exist. Such reserves as were available (including the Guards Division) were not ordered to move until the next day, and were given no orders to intervene until the 23rd. Even those orders were confused. The Division, together with two other reserve divisions, were only in time to ward off two devastating counter-attacks by the Germans.

It was not until 2 a.m. on the 22nd that the Battalion was

ordered towards the fighting. By then they knew that, so far from taking part in a breakthrough, things had gone seriously wrong. So much was clear from the succession of orders and counter-orders that trickled through from Corps Headquarters. The real situation, unknown to the commanders at battalion, or brigade, level, was that the enemy was counter-attacking with increasing success. The quick advance of the British on 20 November had left them in a salient about 8 miles wide and 5 miles deep. But without the needed reserves, the new line was too thinly held, especially on the flanks, and it was on the hinges of the salient that the Germans now directed well executed counter-attacks. The first fell on the northern hinge, in the area of Bourlon Wood; the second was to fall to the south, towards Gouzeaucourt, seven days later. There is no doubt that the Guards Division played the major part in blunting both these attacks, especially the second.

Very heavy fighting took place in the Bourlon Wood area, and although the Welsh Guards were in close support, they were not directly engaged. By 27 November, after four days of confused and bitter fighting, the line was stabilized and the Division was withdrawn for rest. It was not to be for long.

At 9.30 a.m. on 30 November, when the Battalion was still taking it easy at Trescault, the Adjutant, Captain Devas, got the news that the Germans had made their second attack on the salient at Banteux and broken through to Gouzeaucourt, a distance of about three miles. Otherwise information was meagre.

Just before midday the whole of 3rd Guards Brigade moved to Bois Dessart. They then marched back across country to a position just south of Trescault, where they had started from. The country was rolling and down-like, and from their hillside they could see 1st Guards Brigade attacking towards Gouzeaucourt, which they recaptured.

They waited on the bleak hillside until dark. Greatcoats and blankets had been dumped and it was bitterly cold, with a bright moon and a frosty wind. A little comfort was provided by the cookers which came up with a hot meal. At about 8 p.m. the Commanding Officer, Lieutenant-Colonel Gordon, was sent for by the Brigade Commander, who told him that 1st Guards Brigade had been successful and that the Battalion would not be wanted that night. But at midnight he was suddenly sent for again and given the briefest of orders. The Brigade was to capture the Gonnelieu ridge and the high ground to the south of it. The Welsh Guards would have the Grenadiers on their left; on their right would be 2nd Guards Brigade. Eleven tanks would co-operate; time of attack, 6.30 a.m. A couple more paragraphs gave details of artillery targets and boundaries.

Time was now getting on. At a brief conference with his company commanders, Lieutenant-Colonel Gordon ordered Nos 3 and 4 Companies to make up the first wave, No 2 Company the second; Prince of Wales Company would be in reserve. There was just time for a brief reconnaissance of the start-line, a railway embankment, and for the companies to form up, when the order was given for the advance. By now the moon had gone down and it was misty. None of the promised tanks had turned up, and the companies plunged up the hill into the darkness.

Because there had been no time for a proper reconnaissance in daylight, and because there were even no proper maps, it was not appreciated that behind the apparent crest of the objective was a slight depression. In the depression, and covering the false crest, the Germans had posted a number of heavy machine guns. As the leading companies approached the false crest, they were caught, first in the light of star-shells, and then in a whirlwind of fire beyond anything so far experienced in the war. Of the 370 men in the attacking waves, 248 were down in three minutes, of whom 57 were killed. Only Prince of Wales Company were still untouched.

The din was so tremendous that the Commanding Officer and his second-in-command, Major Humphrey Dene, had to shout into each other's ears to make themselves heard. Then, out of the queer half-light of a misty dawn lit by star-shells, came a long line of dazed, blood-covered, crying and cursing men, the survivors and wounded stumbling back.

Lieutenant Arthur Gibbs, in command of Prince of Wales Company, was ordered to take up a position below the crest and send back any unwounded men he could find to reform by the railway. He was lucky enough to find some trenches near the spot and put his men into them.

A little later Dene went up the hill to view the situation. It was now rather lighter, the mist was lifting and visibility was about 300 yards. Dene and Gibbs peered cautiously over the trench, and in the dip between the false and real crest they saw a solitary tank cruising very slowly up and down the enemy line. Shells were falling round it, but its own guns were blazing, and best of all, the Germans were beginning to run away, making for a trench behind them. As the tank turned towards the trench, Gibbs, choosing his moment, got two of his platoons up in support of the tank, without casualties, and relieved the tank of 200 prisoners who were clustering round it with their hands up.

Gibbs then manned the trench, the tank remaining with him until the Coldstream came up on his left. The line was now held by the whole of Prince of Wales Company, the remains of No 4 and 25 men from No 2. There is no doubt that the success of the advance was largely due to the skill and courage of the crew of this solitary tank.

At about 11 a.m. the Brigadier visited the line and decided that nothing further could be done. That night the position was reinforced by the Grenadiers, and during the next three days the Battalion was gradually withdrawn.

On balance the British gained some ground at Cambrai, but the importance of the battle lay not in a few captured acres, but in the development of the tactics which both sides would use in the attack in the following year. Both sides returned to the element of surprise by using no, or only very limited, preliminary bombardment. The Germans used their infantry in small, flexible groups, infiltrating the weak spots in their opponents' defence and then flooding through the gaps; the British used their tanks in mass, with close infantry support, though the tanks, because the British commanders were never given enough of them, never gave the decisive edge which they could have done.

Winter 1917–18: Arras, the Line—the German Offensive

A week after being withdrawn from Cambrai, the Battalion was sent to Arras for a much needed refit. In common with the rest of the Guards Division, the accumulated casualties of Ypres, followed by Cambrai, had been severe, not only in overall numbers, but in trained and experienced NCOs and men; these had to be continually reshuffled between platoons and companies, with a resulting loss of efficiency. Major-General Fielding, commanding the Division, reported that the level of training in the Division, for the time being, could not be regarded as a high one.

The period granted for rest and retraining was not to be long; but in the weeks available, battalions were re-organized, new drafts settled in, and they soon regained their usual pitch of efficiency. They could also relax in billets that were warm, dry and reasonably comfortable (the Welsh Guards were in the town prison). If their address was not a good one, with the almost peace-time amenities of Arras easily available, the Battalion enjoyed a good Christmas.

The Battalion first went into the line again on 1 January, about five miles east of Arras. The position was on a spur north of the River Scarp, and with the exception of one tour was the one they were to hold until March. They were in the line six times in ten weeks, usually for four days at a time.

Defence tactics had changed since the previous year. The line now consisted of a series of outposts, 800 or 1,000 yards in advance of 'the main line of resistance', itself two or three lines of trenches according to the state of work. Finally there was a rear zone in which reserves were concentrated. As few men as possible held the outpost line, and both outpost and main line were strongly supported by machine guns.

At first the weather was bitterly cold, dry and the ground frozen. The trenches appeared adequate and well dug, if not very well sited. A fortnight later, on the Battalion's second tour in the line, the weather changed; it grew warmer, it poured with rain, and the result was disastrous. The trenches were simply washed away, the walls collapsing so suddenly that men had to be dug out.

Work was therefore hard. As well as holding the line, there were nightly fatigues to reconstruct the trenches, lug up material for revetting, and improve the strength and siting of the position. There was an added urgency to this work. Russia was now out of the war, and the Germans were rapidly transferring troops to the Western Front. To be successful a German attack had to be launched soon, before the American forces in France had built up to their full strength.

And as February became March, the signs of a great offensive began to multiply as enemy patrols became more active and their shelling more intense. Warnings to battalions from the staff to be on the alert became more and more agitated. There were two false alarms, and the waiting soldiers began to wonder if the High Command were not crying wolf. On the 15th the Battalion went back into the line again; on the 19th they were relieved for a month's rest and training. On the 21st the storm broke and the Germans attacked with 68 divisions on a front of 54 miles, from Arras in the north to Soissons in the south.

During the next six days the Guards Division came under heavy attack. Twice the situation appeared so critical that substantial withdrawals of five miles were ordered. In the event these were limited, on the left to about 2,000 yards, losing Boyelles; and on the right they had to swing back twice that distance, behind Hamelincourt, to keep contact with a more general retreat. Only six miles away the Germans had broken through completely. During this period the Battalion was mostly in reserve and were only involved in a few skirmishes. But on the night of the 27th they relieved the 1st Grenadiers on the extreme left of the Division. The next day the enemy reopened its attack at 7 a.m. with a violent bombardment, which drove back the division on the Battalion's left and exposed the flank of Prince of Wales Company. But they were able to block their trench, while the open ground was cleared by the Lewis guns. That night a short withdrawal was ordered, again to conform with flanking troops.

Two days later the enemy tried again. This time their artillery and machine gun fire was supported by 14 aircraft, which straffed the British trenches. The attack flooded out from behind Boyelles, in blobs of three or four men, dodging from cover to cover. It was a skilful and determined assault, which reached the Grenadiers' trenches on the Battalion's right, gradually lapping round the Welsh Guards. The attack was driven off by a storm of accurate rifle and machine gun fire, and a prisoner stated that the attacking battalions had been virtually annihilated. The attack was not renewed, and on the 31st the Guards Division was relieved.

There had been withdrawals, but no breakthrough, on the Arras front. But the Germans had come close to winning the war. By 25 March they had to the south broken through to a depth of 40 miles on a 40-mile front. But instead of reinforcing their success, they wasted their reserves against the stubborn bastion of Arras. Their chance slipped away. The Guards Division could be proud of the part they played in 3rd Army's fine performance.

3 THE GREAT WAR:
ADVANCE TO VICTORY

After 5 April the Battalion spent a further ten days either holding the line or in reserve, when the Guards Division was withdrawn into 3rd Army reserve. They had had nearly a month of hectic fighting with no change of clothing and little opportunity to wash. It was a tattered band of scarecrows that marched back to billets in Fosseux. One of the company commanders, Major Dudley-Ward, complained: 'I have men now who are ragged about the trousers to the extent of indecency, and many have their bare toes sticking through their boots.'

For the next four months they settled into the now familiar routine of front line, reserve, and rest for training, refitting and recreation. Reinforcements were getting scarce, and from now on the Battalion was usually under strength. In September reinforcements ceased altogether.

In July 15 officers and 85 NCOs and men from the American 80th Infantry Division were attached under instruction, and the Battalion were impressed by their alertness and their keenness to learn. Their arrival was celebrated by a special issue of whisky sent by Divisional Headquarters. Later, on 15 August, these new friends proved their mettle when they decisively beat off an attack on a post they were holding in 3rd Guards Brigade sector.

This was the start of an often close co-operation between the Guards Division and the Americans. Over the next few weeks they not only relieved each other in the line, but on occasion American battalions came under command of a Guards Brigade, and vice versa.

Meanwhile the German attacks, which had started in March, continued against both the French and British armies. But on 18 July the French delivered a great counter-stroke on the Marne, towards Rheims; and on 8 August a similar blow by the British on the Somme had sent the Germans reeling. It was this battle that the German Chief-of-Staff, Ludendorf, described as the 'black day of the German army'. The reversal of fortune was dramatic: from March to July the initiative had seemed to lie entirely with the Germans; from 8 August it was to lie with the Allies. In their desperation to win the war before the full strength of the Americans could be brought to bear against them, the Germans had used up all their reserves; by contrast the Allies now had at their disposal a growing number of unwearied American divisions. The German soldier on the ground continued to resist stoutly, but his High Command knew that the war was lost; worse, it had lost the will to win.

The final advance can be divided into two parts. The first was the advance in which the British closed up to the Hindenburg Line, over desolate, ruined country which had been fought over for the better part of four years. Muddy, littered with trenches and strongpoints that had been dug and re-dug as the battles had lurched back and forth, it was easily defensible. Then after the Hindenburg Line was breached, came the pursuit. The advancing troops found themselves, for the first time, in unspoiled country where the obstacles were natural ones, strengthened only by the hastily-thrown-up defences of a retreating army.

In between these two phases the last great set-piece battle against an organized defence system was successfully fought, when the Canal du Nord was crossed and the Hindenburg Line shattered.

St Leger

So far the successful attacks of the British and French armies had been to the south of the Somme. In the middle of August it was decided to switch the pressure further north, towards Mauberge. This responsibility fell to 3rd Army, which included the Guards Division. On 15 August the Welsh Guards moved into the reserve area of Blairville, east of Cambrai. They would be operating just north of the battles of the previous autumn.

On 23 August 2nd Guards Brigade attacked from Hamelincourt and advanced 4,000 yards towards St Leger, and that evening the Battalion took over the line in the area of Judas Farm.

On the 24th, at 1 a.m., the Welsh Guards were ordered to attack towards Ecoust, by-passing St Leger to the north. At 7 a.m. the barrage came down and No 3 Company led off on a front of 850 yards. (This width of front for a single company immediately shows a change from the close-order tactics of previous years.) They were under fire from the start, but in their open formation they made good progress. Indeed, they pressed forward too enthusiastically; at one moment they moved into their own barrage and had to draw back for 15 minutes. After being reorganized by Captain Ellis, they continued their advance along the line of a railway, captured a field gun and some prisoners, and passed round to the north of St Leger. They finally reached a trench called St Leger Reserve; here there was a check from machine gun fire and also shelling with mustard gas. Orders were then received that there would be no further advance that day, and the position was consolidated.

The advance was to continue at 4.30 a.m. the next morning, supported by tanks. But a heavy mist had descended which reduced visibility to ten yards. The tanks were unable to turn up, but No 2 Company crept forward and got in among some advance posts with the bayonet, when any further advance was held up by heavy machine gun fire and thick wire. Small parties of the enemy kept looming up through the fog and were driven off.

Prince of Wales Company had also inched forward, but went too far along the railway line and somehow found themselves on the left of No 2 Company instead of behind them and in support. They also were held up by wire and heavy machine gun fire, suffering a number of casualties.

Meanwhile Major Bonn, temporarily in command of the Battalion (Dene had been wounded), had become worried about the situation and decided to go forward to see for himself what was going on. But he, too, was defeated by the mist and found himself behind the German lines.

Gradually the fog thinned. No 4 Company edged forward and secured a strong position on the right flank, and Bonn groped his way back through the German army at about the same time as an order came forward that there was to be no further advance that day.

During the two days' fighting, the Battalion's casualties had been 144, which showed that, however despairing the German High Command might be about the outcome of the war, the German soldier on the ground was still prepared to fight for every inch of ground that he was forced to give up. However the Welsh Guards had done well. In spite of the fact that the troops on their left had not advanced, and in spite of the fog and non-arrival of the tanks on the second day, they had cleared and held the ground in front of them to a depth of 1,000 yards.

The Canal du Nord

The advance to the Canal du Nord, which would bring the Guards Division up to the Hindenburg Line, started on 2 September when 2nd and 3rd Guards Brigades concentrated at Ecoust. At 5.20 a.m. the next day they attacked behind a barrage, which rolled forward at a rate of 100 yards every four minutes. Although the country was crisscrossed with old trenches, capable of vigorous defence, there was little or no opposition that day. The troops found nothing in front of them except numberless dead horses, a few corpses and a plague of flies. The Guardsmen were cautious, suspecting a trap, some new surprise sprung by a skilful enemy. But it soon became clear that the Germans had retreated and that the task was to follow them as closely and as fast as possible, and by 6.45 a.m. they had advanced 2,000 yards.

During the morning the Battalion, now under command of Lieutenant-Colonel R. E. C. Luxmoore-Ball, reached the village of Lagnicourt and sent forward patrols to some high ground to the east of it. The ridge was unoccupied, and at 1 p.m. the whole Brigade advanced again to the next ridge, where an outpost line was formed for the night. The only opposition was from a little long-range shelling.

The advance over this rolling country, a succession of ridges, continued the next day with No 3 Company leading. They gained another 5,000 yards when they were held up on a ridge east of Boursies by machine gun fire, and the enemy was seen in considerable numbers on the ridge beyond. The Battalion was now closing up on the Canal du Nord, and after their almost free run of the last two days, enemy resistance was stiffening. At 6.30 p.m., 2nd Battalion Scots Guards came up in support, and under cover of an artillery barrage the opposite ridge was finally gained.

It was now 5 September. In the last two days the Guards Division had advanced five miles, and a total of 15 miles since leaving Boyelles on 24 August. They were now in front of the Hindenburg Line as planned, and against the Canal du Nord where it turned south of the line at Havrincourt.

During the succeeding month, which they spent facing the Hindenburg Line, all units of the Guards Division got to know the sector well. Nevertheless the greatest care was taken to plan and rehearse the storming of this last, and very strongly prepared, position of the German Army. The assault was due on 27 September. The task given to the Guards Division was to force the canal, breach the Hindenburg support system, and then secure a ridge of high ground which ran east and northeast of Flesquieres to Premy Chapel.

During the night of the 26/27th the troops moved up to their positions in pouring rain, which caused some delay. But punctually at 5.20 a.m., 2nd Guards Brigade launched their attack across the canal, and by 7 a.m. they had established a bridgehead. By 11 a.m., 1st Guards Brigade had passed through and gained a further 1,000 yards. Both brigades had suffered considerable casualties, first from the Hindenburg Support Line and then from Graincourt, outside their boundary to their left. Graincourt continued to give trouble until about 4.30 p.m. when it was captured by 57th Division, after a desperate resistance by the Germans.

The 1st Battalion, Welsh Guards, crossed the canal at Lock 7, an obvious target for enemy shellfire, but they darted across by sections, miraculously without casualties. They then formed up in support of the 1st Grenadiers and closely followed their advance towards Flesquieres. This was at about 9 a.m.

The battle now became confused. Communications broke down between battalions and brigade, and between brigade and division. Grenadiers and Welshmen worked closely together, but in doing so became inextricably mixed.

At about midday Captain L. F. Ellis, taking advantage of some abandoned trenches running towards Flesquieres, led No 3 Company to the outskirts of the village, where he was eventually joined by Prince of Wales and No 2 Companies. The whole Battalion then secured a line, north of the village, in a sunken road.

The Grenadier and Welsh Guards had now driven a tenuous wedge into the German lines: from Graincourt on the left, German gunners were firing at them over open sights, while any movement beyond Flesquieres drew violent machine gun fire from the right.

It was in the sunken road that Lieutenant-Colonel Luxmoore-Ball met Lord Gort, commanding the Grenadiers. Gort had been held up by a strongpoint in a beet factory, just north of Flesquieres. This he had successfully outflanked. Now he asked for Luxmoore-Ball's assistance in fighting his way further along the ridge, towards Premy Chapel. This was readily agreed by Luxmoore-Ball, who ordered Nos 2 and 3 Companies to advance either side of the ridge and guard the Grenadiers' flanks.

The battle along the ridge was a fierce one. The leading companies got within 50 yards of the Premy defences, but were held by intense machine gun fire. Gort was severely wounded,[1] and Luxmoore-Ball, now senior officer on the spot, decided that no further attempts could be made for the moment. He had no artillery support, the Germans could be seen reinforcing Premy, and with both flanks open, the position of the two battalions was too deep and narrow for comfort. He therefore ordered the battalions to stand fast, a decision which was confirmed by Brigade Headquarters. At 4.30 p.m., the pressure was relieved. On the left Graincourt fell to 57th Division, and 12th Division came up in line on the right. By 7.30 p.m. the whole position was firm enough for the two battalions to be relieved.

The 1st Battalion, Welsh Guards, lost 87 killed and wounded that day, a day of which the Guards Division could be proud. To have stormed the Canal du Nord and cut through the Hindenburg defence system was a considerable feat of arms, and the fact that the part played by the Grenadiers and Welshmen was particularly mentioned by the divisional commander in his despatch was a source of additional satisfaction to those concerned.

[1] For his part in this action, Lord Gort (later to command the BEF in France in 1939–40) was awarded the VC.

Pursuit: St Vaast—River Selle—Bavai

The Welsh Guards now had a week's rest in which to recruit their energy for the final effort which would bring the war to a close. The Battalion was very under strength. Reinforcements had now ceased, and although the official establishment allowed for a battle strength of 642, a battalion strength return of this date shows that they could only muster 399. Companies, reduced from four platoons to three, made up some of the difference by including a Lewis gun in company headquarters, with a couple of sanitary men to work it, and using company headquarters as a fourth platoon.

St Vaast
For the Guards Division the last phase of the war started on 8 October. At 5.20 a.m. that morning, the leading divisions of VI Corps had attacked towards Seranvilliers, and a long line of prisoners shuffling to the rear gave the first indication of their success. The next day the Guards Division, which had been in reserve, took over the pursuit. The Germans fought a number of brisk rearguard actions in the course of their retreat, but 1st and 2nd Guards Brigades, who were in the lead, made good progress, and by 10 October had established an outpost line just short of St Hilaire.

On the night of the 10th, 3rd Guards Brigade had orders to pass through the two leading brigades and continue the advance. At 1 a.m. they moved to their forming-up place, a road 800 yards to the west of St Hilaire. The Welsh Guards were on the left of the Brigade, which was to advance with three battalions abreast. It was quite quiet as they moved through the string of outposts, passing north of St Hilaire, and over a ridge which separated them from St Vaast. But the enemy was alert, and although it was not yet light, accurate artillery and machine gun fire forced the companies to deploy. Prince of Wales worked round the south-east of the village; No. 4 advanced slowly to the cross-roads to the west of it.

At daybreak the machine gun fire became heavier, and the enemy revealed itself holding a strong position along the railway line to the north of St Vaast. But No 4 Company managed to secure the road west of St Vaast, and No 2 got into it and captured some prisoners. It was now about 7 a.m., but the artillery and machine guns which should have been in close support of the Battalion had not turned up. Without them it proved impossible to shift the enemy, still in strength along the railway line, and also in a malt house north-west of the village.

So matters remained until about 10.30 a.m., when the supporting battery of artillery turned up and Nos 2 and 4 Companies were able to advance again and complete a line on the other side of the village, in spite of heavy shellfire and a strong concentration of gas. There the Battalion dug in for the night. The division on their left had not kept pace with their advance, and with the railway line still held by the Germans, and also the village of St Aubers behind it, further progress was not possible.

Air reconnaissance next morning suggested that the enemy had withdrawn from St Aubers, and patrols discovered that they had retired to some high ground northeast of St Vaast known as 'Arbre de la Femme', which covered the approaches to the River Selle about 2,000 yards behind it. At 3 p.m. the division on the left started to move, and after a preliminary bombardment the Battalion were able to occupy the 'Arbre de la Femme' ridge with all four companies.

That night No 4 Company slipped down to the river with a light bridge which proved just too short for the job. But they discovered a footbridge that was still intact, and also that the river was fordable. Two platoons crossed at once, without being detected by the enemy. But the following morning, machine gun fire and shelling made this small bridgehead untenable, and they withdrew to a more secure position on the west bank of the river. That night, the 13th, the Battalion was relieved and marched back to St Hilaire.

River Selle

After the Welsh Guards were relieved, further small operations were carried out by other battalions in the Division to improve their positions before the river could be crossed in force. Outposts were established on the far bank, bridging material was carried forward, and detailed plans were made. The assault was due on 20 October, as part of a general advance by 3rd Army. The role of the Guards Division was to force the River Selle, capture the high ground behind it, and then push forward to the next river, the Harpies.

On the 19th the Battalion moved forward into its assembly area. The 1st Battalion, Grenadiers, were to lead 3rd Guards Brigade across the river and establish a bridgehead; 2nd Scots Guards and the Welsh Guards were to follow, pass through and capture the ridge beyond.

At 2 a.m. on the 20th a tremendous barrage came down and the advance started. The Grenadiers were punctually across and the bridgehead secured. They captured a few prisoners, but for the most part the Germans had made off as soon as the barrage started.

The Battalion began their move down to the river soon after 2 a.m. Filing over the narrow footbridges was a slow business. The Royal Engineers had placed them earlier in the night, so skilfully and quietly that the enemy had not interrupted their construction. But there were only eight for the whole Division, and two for the Battalion, with the result that the Battalion got very strung out as they threaded their way across. However, soon after 3 a.m. the leading companies, Nos 2 and 4, were over and making for the high ground beyond.

It was a dark night with a misty rain, and they had to struggle up steep, sticky ploughed fields, until at 4.30 a.m. they received a check from machine gun fire, as did the battalions on their right and left. This lasted until shortly after 6.30, when arrangements had been made for additional artillery support. But the enemy's resistance suddenly crumbled, and by 7 a.m. the Battalion had moved forward and secured its objective, the Solesme ridge, which overlooked the next river, the Harpies.

Throughout the day there was considerable shellfire, as well as some heavy gassing. But the Battalion had dug itself in and casualties were surprisingly few. At 6 p.m. orders came through to push forward to the Harpies, and as soon as dusk fell, patrols went out, and by the next morning No 4 Company had established a number of posts along the river bank. The day was spent by the Guards Division in re-organizing and improving their positions, with little interference from the enemy, and on the night of 21/22 October they were relieved.

Bavai

After their relief the Guards Division spent the remainder of the month in rest billets. The area in which they found themselves was almost undamaged. Villages provided houses and barns with sound roofs and walls, and the soldiers could make themselves comfortable. Rest meant rest; training and parades took place, but there were none of the back-breaking fatigues to be carried out almost nightly in mud up to the knees, or deeper, and under incessant shellfire.

This change in circumstances made the change in the fortunes of war obvious. But to the soldier on the ground the well-fought rearguard actions of the German fighting soldier gave little indication of the swift outcome. Hope was in the air, however—even an odd sort of gaiety. As the Battalion marched towards Villers Pol on the night of 2 November, from the roads on either side of them they heard the sound of music. Regiments were jaunting forward to the brass of their bands. The Welshmen sang.

Valenciennes had been taken and on 4 November the Guards Division were to open the final advance towards Bavai and Mauberge. The plan allowed for a forward leap of seven miles; the days were gone when these calculations were made in yards. Zero hour had been fixed for 6 a.m. It was a dark, wet night; 1st and 2nd Guards Brigades, who were leading, had to feel their way forward. With daylight the rain turned to fog; but timings were maintained and by 6 p.m. a line had been reached east of Preux-au-Sart, in spite of a couple of brisk engagements on the way.

Meanwhile the Battalion, in reserve with 3rd Guards Brigade, were making their way forward over roads choked with all the panoply of a victorious army; motor and horse-drawn transport of every kind, guns, ambulances and marching men. That evening they reached Amfroipret, where they got orders to take over the advance the following day, towards Bavai and Mauberge.

At Amfroipret they came under considerable shelling, suffering the greatest misfortune when a single shell hit a barn, killing or wounding 31 men of No 4 Company and reducing their already low strength by about half. However Major Dudley-Ward, who was commanding the Battalion, kept to his original plan and ordered No 4 to lead on the next morning and capture the village of Bouvignies.

The attack started at 5 a.m. No 2 Company advanced along the line of the railway to Bavai; No 4, on their left, in spite of weakness in numbers, occupied Bouvignies without much trouble, and took up a position on the far side across the Bavai road.

Captain L. F. Ellis then formed up No 3 Company, on the east side of Bouvignies, and attacked towards Prehert Farm, which lay on the other side of the railway. Finding his platoons held up in the hedged fields just short of the line, which ran through the cutting, he went forward to find out the reason for the delay. He was told that the cutting was full of Germans. Expressing disbelief, he ran impatiently on, jumped into the cutting and found himself facing a party of about 30 Germans. Armed only with a walking stick he could do nothing but wave it at the startled enemy. Luckily for Ellis he had been followed by Corporal Gordon and

Lance-Sergeant W. Jones, both excellent shots, and before the Germans could take to their heels, 11 of them had been accounted for.

The whole Company now followed and came tumbling into the cutting; but without giving them pause for breath, Ellis led them up and over the opposite bank. They found themselves in a field which rose in a gentle slope, at the top of which the enemy were manning a line of slit-trenches. Again without pause Ellis led his men forward in a series of short rushes, bundled the Germans out of their cover and continued on to Prehert Farm. There followed a hide-and-seek fight until the farm, its outbuildings and orchards were cleared.

Prince of Wales Company now came up on Ellis's left flank, which allowed him to continue on towards the Bavai road. This was a much slower process involving working down the hedgerows; besides Ellis no longer had sufficient men for further adventures. But he manoeuvred his Company forward until he was ordered to stand fast. No 2 Company also moved up, and by that night the Battalion had sent patrols into Bavai, and Prince of Wales Company had established a platoon on the outskirts. It was the Welsh Guards' last fight; their casualties were 94.

The following day the advance was resumed by 1st and 2nd Guards Brigades and progress was rapid. Early in the morning of 10 November Mauberge fell to the 1st Brigade. And it was at Mauberge at 7 a.m. that instructions regarding a ceasefire for 11 a.m. that day, 11 November, reached the Headquarters of the Guards Division.

Armistice

The Armistice was confirmed to the Welsh Guards at the little village of Douzies. At long last the enemy was decisively defeated. After four long years of slaughter, victory seemed almost an anticlimax. The entry in the Battalion's war diary is brief: 'News reached the Battalion that an armistice had been signed to take effect at 11.00 hours to-day.' At home there was dancing and singing in the streets; but for the troops in the field, nothing but relief. They spent the day resting—and cleaning their kit. After all, the next morning, as the diary also records, there would be Battalion parade.

In the rejoicing and the relief, the British Army and its commanders never got the credit they deserved for their last brilliant, fast-moving campaign, which had broken the Germans, kept them on the run and hounded them back to their own frontiers.

For the Guards Division the achievement of that campaign was an advance of 50 miles against a skilful and still determined enemy. They had had little rest. In the 81 days since leaving Moyenville, 54 days had been spent in the line, and 29 of those had been days of hard fighting. It is a proud record. But the brilliance was forgotten, swamped in the memory of the mud and the killing in the years that preceded it.

During the three years that the 1st Battalion, Welsh Guards, fought in France, of the 3,853 men who served with it, 856 were killed and 1,755 were wounded. And of those who went to France with the Battalion in August 1915, only 13 served from first to last, without interruption, to return home unscathed.

'You have no traditions,' a young officer from an older regiment had once said, 'No past'. That might have been true in 1915. But three years of intense fighting had crammed a past into the new regiment, and bred a tradition fully up to the standards of the Brigade of Guards.

INTERLUDE:
BETWEEN THE WARS 1919-1939

The Battalion's service abroad was not quite over. After a few pleasant days in Mauberge, where they were fêted by the townspeople, they set off on the long march to Cologne. The march was an arduous one, 112 miles through the steep country of the Ardennes, over poor roads and in bad weather. Cologne was reached on 20 December, and there the Battalion remained as part of the Army of Occupation until March.

Although they were comfortable enough, and the routine was not demanding, it was nevertheless a testing time. The war was over; at home, and in the Army itself, there was an understandable cry for rapid demobilization. Great steadiness and discipline were required to achieve the standards of smartness and morale which an army occupying a defeated country must display. The example of the Guards Division was to be invaluable.

At last, on 11 March 1919, the Welsh Guards sailed for home. They embarked, proudly, at Dunkirk; none of them could have foreseen the very different circumstances under which they would leave the same shore 21 years later.

On 22 March the Guards Division marched triumphantly through London, the salute being taken by the King outside Buckingham Palace. Demobilized officers and men followed their battalions in plain clothes, and wounded men unable to walk were carried in lorries. The regiment was commanded by Colonel Murray-Threipland, now Regimental Lieutenant-Colonel, followed by Lieutenant-Colonels Gordon and Dene as previous Battalion commanders in France, riding abreast. The Battalion itself was commanded by Lieutenant-Colonel Luxmoore-Ball.

The Welsh Guards had proved themselves in war; they now had to prove themselves up to the no less exacting standards of the Brigade of Guards in peacetime. Almost at once a crisis of the first magnitude arose. Among the huge and inevitable postwar cuts, there was a strong effort, led by the Major-General of the day, to disband both the Irish and the Welsh Guards. He was supported in this bid by the Secretary of State for War, Mr Winston Churchill, who was to become Prime Minister in the Second World War.

Happily both regiments were able to resist this manoeuvre. The Prime Minister of the time was a Welshman, Mr Lloyd George; and any lingering doubts about the Regiment's survival were dispersed by the King's appointment of the Prince of Wales as Colonel of the Regiment on 3 June 1919. But it was to be a long and exacting task for the young regiment to establish itself as the equal to the best of the Brigade of Guards. In this short account, of those who contributed to the result, which stood the test of the Second World War, two must stand for the rest.

The first was Regimental Sergeant-Major Stevenson, MBE, DCM, MM. Very few of the warrant and non-commissioned officers had served before the war. And with the return of the Battalion to London and ceremonial duties, 'There was hardly a man who could so much as roll a cape correctly.' It was 'Stevo' who, almost alone, drove the Battalion to the high standard required, with a combination of discipline, understanding—and humour: throwing his pace-stick in the air, and falling on his knees on the barrack square, 'Allah,' he would enquire, 'who will save me from these horrible men?' But even he was satisfied when the Battalion first trooped its Colour in 1928. The other was

47

Interlude: Between the Wars 1919–1939

Lieutenant-Colonel M. B. Beckwith-Smith, who became Commanding Officer in October 1932. He took in hand the Battalion's field training, and with quiet insistence instilled the realism and skills which were to pay off so well only a few years later. The debt which the Regiment owes to these two men is beyond measure.

Two other features, curious to any but a Welshman, contributed to the confidence of the adolescent regiment: singing and rugby football. A choir was started almost at once, which soon helped to make the Regiment known in Wales by winning a number of competitions. Similarly the rugby team was successful almost from the first, gaining their first Army Cup in the season 1922/23.

Finally there was the Colonelcy of the Prince of Wales. His interest and support were more than formal; close, active and direct, they did much to provide an identity and to stiffen the determination to do well.

Unlike the Guardsman of today, his predecessor saw little service abroad in peacetime. With the exception of a two-year tour in Egypt from 1929, the 20 years between the wars were spent at home. But the rise of Hitler to power in Germany in the early thirties already pointed to the war which broke out in 1939. As part of a belated and modest expansion of the army, the Welsh Guards were ordered to raise a second battalion. They formed initially at Chelsea Barracks in May 1939. Meanwhile, in the previous month, the 1st Battalion had sailed for Gibraltar.

4 THE SECOND WORLD WAR: 1939-1943

When, at the end of the Great War, the peace treaty was signed, Marshal Foch, who had led the Allied armies in France, forecast with uncanny accuracy another war in 20 years' time. Indeed the seeds were sown almost at once. The Allies occupied too little of Germany, so that too few Germans actually saw the armies of their conquerors, while the German armies were allowed to march home apparently intact. The myth immediately started that they had not been defeated, but betrayed by communists or Jews.

When Hitler, leader of the Nazi Party, became Chancellor of Germany, he fostered the legend with care. It suited his policy of aggression. He wished, not only to avenge the defeat of 1918, but also to found a German Empire which, he boasted, would last for a thousand years. He soon set about realizing his ambitions. In 1935 he reoccupied the Rhineland, which under the Treaty of Versailles was to remain demilitarized. In 1938 he swallowed Austria and part of Czechoslovakia, and in 1939 the rest of Czechoslovakia. In each case he was unopposed, except for diplomatic protest.

In Great Britain and France, by contrast, memories of the holocaust of 1914–18 were still vivid and public opinion was strongly anti-war. Little was spent on defence. The French, it is true, built an enormous, static fortification along their frontier, called the Maginot Line. But this military white elephant was out of date as soon as it was built. Moreover it ended 120 miles from the sea, and when the time

49

came was duly outflanked by Germany's modern, mobile forces. who went around the side!!

Unlike the Great War, the Second World War was largely one of movement. The tank came into its own; ironically, because it was a British invention, it was the Germans, defeated in 1918, who developed its full potential. Combined with close air support, backed by mobile infantry and artillery and good communications, the tank dominated the battlefield as the machine gun and barbed wire had dominated the fighting 20 years before.

After Hitler had occupied Czechoslovakia it became plain that the next victim of Germany's expansion would be Poland. At the last moment Great Britain and France faced up to this unrestrained ambition, guaranteeing Poland's independence against German aggression. Thinking, with some reason, that this obligation would not be honoured, Hitler invaded Poland on 1 September 1939. On the 3rd the British and French governments declared war on Germany. The next day the British Expeditionary Force started to cross over to France. Its Headquarters was set up at Arras.

From September 1939 until May 1940, the period of the 'Phoney War', the armies of Britain and France were scarcely engaged against the Germans. The French lurked behind their massive fortification; the British, with pick and shovel, were trying to provide some sort of defence for the 120-mile gap between the Maginot Line and the sea.

These unexciting months ended abruptly on the 10 May 1940, when the German Army was unleashed in a whirlwind campaign which in three weeks saw the capitulation of Holland, followed by Belgium, and the withdrawal of a British army from the Continent of Europe, to be crowned after a further week by the surrender of France.

In the early hours of that day the Germans opened their assault with air attacks on a number of key cities and airfields in Holland, Belgium and France, including the British Headquarters at Arras. The following day the German ground forces invaded Holland. The assault was so swift that there was not even time for the dykes to be opened and the land flooded, the traditional delay imposed on an invader. Any effective resistance was over in three days, and on the 14th the Dutch Government surrendered.

Meanwhile on the 12th the Germans had invaded Belgium, with the same devastating results. The British and French armies moved forward in support, but the Germans were already making good speed through Luxembourg and the Ardennes. On 15 May they crossed the Meuse and struck deep into France.

The BEF thus found themselves with both flanks exposed. There was no recourse but to withdraw towards their original positions on the Franco–Belgian frontier. But the Germans were still swinging behind them, and on the 20th reached the coast at Abbeville, leaving a corridor, still for the moment free, which led up to the Channel ports of Boulogne and Calais. At the southern end of the corridor stood Arras, lying across the centre of a network of roads and railways which supported the BEF, and so guarding all their communications.

1940: 1st Battalion, Arras—Dunkirk

With the outbreak of war the 1st Battalion were not to be left for long in Gibraltar. On 7 November they sailed for Marseille, and after a ceremonial march through Paris they left for Arras. There they took up their role, the protection of GHQ, which was quartered in and around the town which they had fought so hard to defend 22 years before.

Although Arras had been bombed during the opening stages of the campaign, it was not until 17 May that the town became directly threatened by the enemy's ground forces, and the Battalion was ordered to take up positions to defend it. As they marched through, they saw for the first time the pathetic streams of refugees searching for shelter, which was to become such a common and distressing sight during the operations of the next two weeks.

The other troops allocated to the defence of Arras were a scratch lot: a hurriedly formed squadron of tanks, some sappers, military police, and men on leave, who had been stranded and were unable to get back to their units.

By that evening the Battalion had established itself in positions on the outskirts of Arras. Prince of Wales Company (under Sir William Makins) was on the Doullens road to the west; No 2 Company (Captain J. E. Gurney) faced south on the Bapaume–Cambrai road; and No 4 Company (Captain M. E. C. Smart) guarded a couple of bridges to the north. The Carrier and Mortar Platoons were left in reserve to be used as required. Road-blocks were constructed, protected by mines, slit-trenches were dug, and houses were loop-holed and sand-bagged.

The next two nights passed without incident, but on the 19th all troops not necessary to the defence of Arras, including Rear HQ, BEF, were ordered to leave. That day, from the air at least, the attack on Arras started in earnest, and the Battalion saw for the first time the results of concentrated bombing. The station was badly hit, and with it two train-loads of refugees, with sickening consequences.

On the 20th the real pressure against the town started, with German attacks against the companies' road-blocks. Enemy armoured cars first tried their luck against No 2 Company, but the leading cars blew up on the mines, and two more were destroyed by platoon weapons.

On the northern outskirts an attack by lorried infantry was driven off by No 4 Company, and to the east and south-west, reconnaissance parties were broken up by mortar fire. It will be seen that with these probing attacks coming from so many points of the compass, Arras was in a fair way to being surrounded. Later in the day an even more determined attack was driven off by a platoon of No 2 Company, under command of Lieutenant W. H. R. Llewellyn, with the help of a few of the tanks.

Tension was briefly relieved the next day when a British counter-attack went in to the northeast of Arras, with great local success; 400 prisoners were captured. But the French, who were meant to have co-operated with a similar attack, did not move. The garrison was little better off than it had been; indeed, for the first time they came under shellfire. Air attack also increased and casualties began to mount. They hung on for two more days when the Commander-in-Chief, Lord Gort, gave orders for the town to be evacuated.

The Battalion was due to start moving just before dawn on the 24th, and to avoid detection, companies were to move independently towards Douai. They were lucky in that an early morning mist cloaked their movement, and for the most part they slipped away unseen. But about three miles out from the town the Battalion transport, under the Quartermaster (Lieutenant J. C. Buckland), found its way blocked by the column ahead, which had obviously been halted by the heavy firing which could now be heard through the mist. Guarding the transport was a section of the Carrier Platoon and a troop of light tanks under Lieutenant the Hon. Christopher Furness. Furness told Buckland to turn his vehicles and get out as quickly as possible. But Buckland pointed out that it would take too long, and that with the mist rising he would be caught defenceless by the enemy.

Furness then promised to keep the enemy occupied long enough for Buckland to extricate himself. Although he had been wounded the night before, Furness then set off with his small force. He appreciated that long-range action would be insufficient to distract the enemy for his purpose, and that he must engage them at close quarters. Advancing with his three carriers, and supported by the tanks, he then proceeded to drive round the enemy position several times at close range, inflicting severe loss. But heavy fire from the enemy gradually took its toll; first the three tanks were

C

knocked out. Then, one by one, the three carriers, most of their crews being killed or wounded. When finally his own carrier was disabled and the bren-gunner killed, Furness dismounted and, wounded as he was, engaged the enemy in hand-to-hand combat, until he too was killed. The fierceness of his attack and his self-sacrifice allowed the column of vehicles, as well as many others, to get away without loss. For this supreme action Furness was awarded the Victoria Cross.

For the next four days the Battalion retreated: to Wazier, to Premesque, and to Cassel, now the location of GHQ and which was in danger of being surrounded. But for the time being the Welsh Guards drove off any attempts to penetrate the line. From Cassel they were ordered to Hautkerque, and then back to Cassel, which was again under attack. There was now no disguising the fact that, if the British Army was to live to fight another day, they must somehow get back to the coast, and from there return to England.

From Cassel the Battalion was ordered to another threatened flank, at Vyfweg–West Capel. They arrived in darkness, following a long struggle through roads choked with refugees, troops and transport. But that night, 28 May, they were able to organize themselves in a roughly triangular position, with the base running from Vyfweg to West Capel, and facing the enemy at Soex. The apex was near Ratte Ko to the northeast. The companies were very spread out; between No 2 Company at West Capel and 48th Division near Rexpoede, there was a gap of two miles.

That night was comparatively quiet. But the next morning patrols were observed in the vicinity of No 2 Company, and that afternoon it was heavily attacked by tanks and infantry from the southwest. The brunt of this first attack fell on No 5 Platoon, under Lieutenant Llewellyn, and both he and several of his men were wounded. It was soon clear that they would not be able to hang on for very long, and Captain Gurney, the Company Commander, withdrew them to the grounds of the moated château, which he had made his headquarters.

On the northern edge of the village, No 6 Platoon, under Platoon Sergeant-Major Maisey, was also attacked and cut off from the château. The enemy were held off for a time, but after heavy mortaring, tanks got into the village and No 6 Platoon was overrun. There was some close-quarter fighting, but the tanks drove over the slit-trenches. Those who were not crushed were buried.

Although he did not know it, Captain Gurney's position was even more dangerous than he could have imagined. On his left, 48th Division had been ordered to withdraw; on his right, Prince of Wales and Headquarter Companies were under attack in Vyfweg, and so was No 3 Company behind him. At one time enemy tanks reached the road between Vyfweg and Ratte Ko and overran part of Brigade Head-quarters. They were driven off by a battery of Royal Horse Artillery; both this battery and the Fife and Forfarshire Yeomanry who were in support, gave the Battalion the most magnificent help until the end.

At about six o'clock in the evening, the Welsh Guards were ordered to the coast. The Yeomanry covered their flank, the battery of R.H.A. firing the last of its ammunition in their support, before they too were ordered back to the beaches. Most of the Battalion got away without too much trouble, but No 2 Company was by then surrounded and unable to move, at any rate in daylight. So they fought on in the château until, at last, night fell.

One by one they managed to slip through a hole in the wall and collect in a nearby ditch. At first they had not been seen but, when they opened fire on an approaching body of enemy, it was evident from the return fire, which came from all directions, that the immediate area was crawling with Germans. In twos and threes the gallant remnant of 2 Company threaded their way through the German patrols and into open country. It was a much depleted party, 19 unwounded and four wounded, that Captain Gurney finally led to the coast, where he found the Commanding Officer and the rest of the Battalion, waiting patiently among the sand dunes for evacuation. They arrived home, at Sheerness, in a paddle-steamer.

1940: 2nd Battalion—Boulogne

At the outbreak of war the newly-formed 2nd Battalion was stationed at the Tower of London, and on 14 February 1940 received its colours from King George VI. Training facilities at the Tower were limited; it was not until March that the Commanding Officer, Lieutenant-Colonel Sir Alexander Stanier, was able to get them away for some intensive training at Camberley. There they were brigaded with 2nd Battalion, Irish Guards, to form 20th Guards Brigade, under Brigadier Fox-Pitt, himself a Welsh Guardsman.

They trained hard for two months until on 11 May both Irish and Welsh Guards were sent away on Whitsun leave, by special trains. But the Germans had already started their *blitzkrieg* through the Low Countries, and the British Government promised the Dutch the assistance of a small force at The Hague. The immediate recall of the battalions was ordered, and some of the special trains were stopped. But it was clear that neither battalion could be at full strength for a day or two. Accordingly a composite battalion was quickly cobbled together and despatched to the Hook of Holland, where they landed on Whit Monday, 13 May. The Welsh Guards' contribution was a strong company of 201 under Captain Heber-Percy.

It was to be a brief stay. They took up positions covering the port, suffered some casualties from heavy bombing, and although paratroops were seen floating down in the distance, no ground attack developed. But the general situation deteriorated so rapidly that the following day the Dutch sued for peace, and after the Dutch Royal Family had crossed to England the Battalion was ordered home. Their real and testing introduction to war was not to be long delayed.

At 11.30 a.m. on 21 May, while out on an exercise, the Battalion was ordered, with 2nd Irish Guards, to proceed overseas that afternoon. They arrived at Dover at midnight, to discover that their destination was Boulogne. They embarked as soon as possible, but because they had been assured that a complete scale of transport, heavy weapons and wireless sets awaited them at Boulogne, they took with them only their personal weapons. When they landed, at ten o'clock the next morning, they found the promise was an empty one. They were even without maps, except for two that were inadequate.

The general situation was that the Germans, having swept through Holland, Belgium and much of northern France, had now swung round and were attacking the Channel Ports from the rear. Boulogne, which is surrounded by a range of low-lying hills, was under increasing pressure from a German armoured division. Although other troops were in the town, the main burden of its defence was to fall on 20th Guards Brigade. The sector given to the 2nd Battalion covered the northeastern approaches; but its front was 6,000 yards wide, and even so there was a gap between its left and the sea.

The day of the 22nd was comparatively free of enemy activity. There was some shelling, and some enemy tanks were seen and driven off, but companies were able to take up their positions without trouble. The following morning brought the first determined enemy attacks. No 2 Company, under Major H. M. C. Jones-Mortimer, had been attacked from the air the day before, and had been under continuous artillery and machine gun fire. After a quiet night the shelling started again, and in the early morning a tank attack developed. It was held for about two hours, but eventually the tanks got their range too accurately and the company had to withdraw behind a railway line. From there they drove off an infantry attack, but the tanks side-stepped and continued to feel their way forward into Boulogne. Headquarter Company and No 3 Company were also attacked, but in spite of stiff resistance found themselves being outflanked as the tanks again side-stepped and got in behind them. In the afternoon the Battalion was ordered to withdraw closer into the town and defend the approaches to the harbour. This was not easy, with the enemy snapping at its heels, and in places already behind it.

In the town itself conditions were chaotic. The press of leaderless soldiers, refugees, fifth columnists and snipers all added to the difficulty of the Commanding Officer in maintaining communication with his companies, and therefore exercising command. Without radio it was only due to the determined efforts of Guardsman T. F. Potter, a despatch rider, that orders got through at all. At six in the evening the Battalion was ordered to withdraw to the quay.

Meanwhile the Navy were sending destroyers into the harbour to take off as many troops as possible, a task that increased in danger as the Germans got their guns into action on the high ground which dominates the town, and bombarded the port. Furthermore mobile detachments of Germans had reached the far side of the harbour, bringing direct small arms fire on to the quay where the Battalion was trying to assemble. It was at about this time, due to mis-information through lack of good communication, that Numbers 2 and 4 Companies, believing that the last ship had gone, tried to break out and embark further down the coast. But their attempt failed and most of them were captured.

Of the rest of the Battalion, most managed to get away in the destroyers. But defiance continued to be shown. Major J. C. Windsor Lewis had also failed to get the order to retire,[1] and when he reached the quay he found the Battalion

[1] In spite of efforts by the Commanding Officer, who personally battered on the door of the house in which Windsor Lewis had barricaded himself. Either he did not hear because of the din, or he was not opening to anyone!

gone. Collecting a scratch force from what he could find of 2 and 4 Companies, some Irish Guardsmen, Engineers and French soldiers, he held out at the railway station for nearly two days, when lack of ammunition, food and water at last forced him to surrender. Although wounded he later managed to escape to England. Three years later he took command of the 2nd Battalion in time to take them back to France after D-Day.

A Long Wait

Both the 1st and 2nd Battalions had played their part in the gallant retreat, and at a high price. Between them the Battalions had lost 72 of all ranks killed. Of the wounded only 88 could be evacuated; 453, including the rest of the wounded, had remained in enemy hands.

The bulk of the Army had been saved, but relief at its safe return tended to disguise the magnitude of the disaster. Few people were aware that if the Army itself was safe, it was almost completely without arms or equipment of any sort. There were few modern tanks, fewer anti-tank guns and radios—there was even a shortage of rifles. Gallantry in retreat does not win wars, and although British forces were soon to be engaged in many other parts of the world, it was to be four years before they were to return to the Continent of Europe—the ultimate objective if Germany was to be defeated.

But before this ambition could be achieved, the country lay in desperate danger of invasion, and evidence of the urgency began to be displayed. The Home Guard, the paladins of 'Dad's Army', was raised, pill-boxes and anti-tank defences appeared in sleepy villages, signposts were removed from cross-roads and road junctions, and place-names were abolished from railway stations. Church bells fell silent, to be used only as a tocsin if an enemy landing should take place—and much later to peal out the news of victory.

Very little lay between the people of Great Britain and disaster. Luckily the German armies, surprised at the speed of their success, needed time to reorganize, and Hitler, believing that the British would recognize defeat and throw their hand in, held back. This delay allowed a few vital weeks. The inspiration of Churchill, now Prime Minister, rallied the spirit of the British people. More important the Royal Air Force was still undefeated, and no invasion could take place until the Luftwaffe had driven it from the skies.

The first round in the Battle of Britain was fought on 8 August, rising to a crescendo on the 17th, and continuing for the rest of the month with almost daily attacks by a thousand to sixteen hundred aircraft. But by the end of the month the Germans had suffered a decisive defeat, their first in the war. Although the air attacks were to continue, and civilian casualties rose to 43,000 killed and 50,000 seriously injured, and although the threat of invasion was to linger on for another two years, a check had been imposed; little by little time was gained.

By autumn the 1st and 2nd Battalions were up to strength, and equipment started to become available. But in the spring of 1941 the decision was taken to form a Guards Armoured Division. The Commander-in-Chief, Home Forces, was told that he should be ready the following spring to meet an invasion by a large number of enemy divisions, including a high proportion of armour. To meet such a force he had such a limited number of armoured divisions at his own disposal that he decided that two infantry divisions must be converted to armour as rapidly as possible. After various deliberations, and after the Major-General commanding the Brigade of Guards had obtained the King's approval, the formation and training of the Guards Armoured Division went ahead as speedily as the availability of new equipment would allow.

Divisional Headquarters was formed in June, and in

September the Division, which included both the 1st and 2nd Battalions, assembled on Salisbury Plain. The 1st Battalion moved from Wimbledon, where they had been since their return from France, to Midsomer Norton, and the 2nd from Byfleet to Codford St Mary.

Both battalions had much to learn, especially the 2nd which now converted to armour. The weather was wet, and most units in the Division moved into half-completed camps, with no hard standings for the mass of transport and tanks which they were beginning to acquire. Their first ventures in their new role that winter left them enthusiastic, if muddy.

In the autumn of 1941, on 24 October, the Holding Battalion, to which men who had completed their preliminary training were posted, was reconstituted as the 3rd Battalion. Their role of providing reinforcements for the other two battalions continued, but a great deal of hard training was achieved over the next 14 months and by the end of 1942 they were a high-quality battalion in their own right. And although the newest, they were to be the first of the Welsh Guards' battalions to re-enter the war.

In 1941 Great Britain acquired a half ally in Soviet Russia, when in July of that year she was invaded by the Germans. Initially the Germans achieved the same swift success as they had in western Europe. The Russians fought bitterly against the common enemy, and by winter the tide had been stemmed, although by the end of the war it became clear that her aims were as entirely selfish and expansionist as those of Hitler himself.

Although invasion was still expected, the possibility was becoming more and more remote. Then on 7 December 1941 the scene changed utterly. On that day the Japanese surprised the American fleet at Pearl Harbor and within weeks had overrun Manilla, Hong Kong, Singapore and Malaya. A few weeks later the whole of South-East Asia was in Japanese hands; India and even Australia were threatened. The speed and scope of the Japanese operations had exceeded anything that even the Germans had yet achieved.

These were great disasters. But the United States of America was now an ally of Great Britain. America was unprepared for war and much hard fighting and many setbacks lay ahead, but her vast resources made a victorious outcome to the war certain.

Meanwhile in the Middle East the fluctuating fortunes of the British forces there had started with the brilliant campaign of General Wavell, who advanced 600 miles, routed the Italian army in North Africa and took 130,000 prisoners. But General Wavell's commitments were too many for the troops he had in hand. Abyssinia, Greece, Crete, Iraq and Syria all fell within his theatre of operations, and his success was reversed. It was not until October 1942, when sufficient resources in men and material could be made available to an Irish Guardsman, General Alexander, that the tide was again turned and the Axis army under General Rommel was hurried back towards Tunisia.

On 8 January 1943 the 3rd Battalion was ordered to mobilize for service overseas, and on 5 February they sailed for North Africa, landing at Algiers eleven days later, under the command of Lt-Col D. E. P. Hodgson.

1943: 3rd Battalion, North Africa—Fondouk

At the end of October 1942 the 8th Army defeated the German and Italian armies at El Alamein and started their drive westward through the Libyan desert. On 8 November an allied army, British and American, landed behind the retreating Germans in Morocco and Algeria. The aim was to destroy completely the enemy forces in North Africa, gain possession of the North African coast, and so provide a jumping-off place for the invasion of southern Europe.

1st Guards Brigade, who had taken part in the initial landings, had had some stiff fighting. Tunisia is a rugged, mountainous country, easily defended, and every inch of ground was sharply contested by the Germans. Casualties in 1st Guards Brigade had been correspondingly severe. 2nd Battalion, the Hampshire Regiment, in particular had been reduced after a rough battle to only 170 men and three officers. Six Welsh Guards officers who had been attached to them were all killed or wounded.

The 3rd Battalion, who had been sent out to replace them, finally joined 1st Guards Brigade on 1 March 1943. For five weeks the Battalion held various positions in the line, without being involved in any heavy fighting, but putting an edge on their training under active service conditions.

By now the 8th Army from the east, and the British–American forces from the west, were approaching each other, with the German forces being increasingly nipped between them. On 7 April 1st Guards Brigade was ordered to capture the Fondouk Gap, which would allow the tanks of 6th Armoured Division to pass through and join up with the 8th Army. The Fondouk Pass, and the road which runs through it, is flanked north and south by steep hills with a loose, stony surface. The objective of the 3rd Battalion was the northern arm, about 700 feet high, and topped by a spine of rock. Called the Djebel ain el Rhorab, this feature is itself divided into two separate features not separately named on the map, but in the battle-shorthand of that day known as 'the Djebel' on the right and 'the Razorback' on the left. At the foot of the Djebel was a dusty, scattered Arab village.

In front of the hills lay open, sandy country, normally with little vegetation, but at this time of year alive with spring flowers: oleander, wild tulips, and blazes of scarlet poppies. The whole area was criss-crossed with small wadis, or water courses, which drain away the winter torrents but which are dry in summer. Running across the Battalion front were two large wadis, the Rhouil and the Marguellil.

On the night of 8 April the Battalion lay behind the

Marguellil, with No 1 Company thrown across as an advance guard in the area of point 252. During the night a patrol was sent out from the Company to see if the Djebel was occupied. It did not return and the Company Commander, Captain R. C. Twining, set out by himself to try to find it. He too failed to return and his body was found the next day beyond the village and part of the way up the hill.

The following morning the Battalion stood-to at five o'clock, and at six-thirty started to move forward. On the right No 2 Company was supported by No 4, and on the left No 3 Company led with No 1 in support. They reached their first objective, the wadi Rhouil, without casualties, and then pushed on to their main objectives, the Djebel and the Razorback. It was then that they attracted the first enemy fire, mortars and machine guns from the hill, and uncomfortably accurate sniping from the Arab village. As the companies continued to advance, casualties increased, until by about eight o'clock they were effectively pinned down in the foothills, about 300 yards from the base of the Djebel. Only a section of No 2 Company, under Lieutenant D. A. N. Allen, managed to work its way forward and upward until it was almost on the objective.

The Commanding Officer therefore decided to try to outflank the position from the left, and No 1 Company (now commanded by Lieutenant A. G. Stewart) was ordered to move round and attack the Razorback from the north, where it falls in a steep shoulder into the maze of wadis. Meanwhile No 4 Company had tried to move up on the right; they too were halted by heavy and continuous fire that now came from the Djebel. All four companies were therefore committed and unable to make any headway. To make matters worse, wireless communication with the companies had broken down.

It was now plain that to capture the objective more support was needed, and to arrange it the Commanding Officer returned from his forward to his rear Headquarters, where he met the Brigade Commander. He asked for and got extra artillery, and the support of a half-squadron of tanks from the Lothian and Border Horse. But the extra support meant a new plan, which had to be communicated to the companies on the ground; and they were strung out in the foothills below the Djebel, out of touch with Battalion Headquarters and with each other.

The success that followed was due to the decisive action and powers of leadership shown by the adjutant, Captain G. D. Rhys-Williams. He had already been round the companies to find out what was happening. He now volunteered to go forward again to explain the plans for the new attack, due to start at one o'clock. It was now midday and time was getting short. Taking the Commanding Officer's carrier, which luckily had a wireless set which worked, he drove off to No 1 Company on the left flank.

The Lothians had meanwhile made a dash for the same spot and arrived under the shoulder of the Razorback and married up with the Company. From there they were able to give covering fire along the top of the ridge and down the forward slope. A little later, as they manoeuvred forward, they were able to fire on to the reverse slope as well, which played a considerable part in eventually forcing the enemy to withdraw.

When Rhys-Williams got to the foot of the Razorback, he had visited Nos 2 and 3 Companies on the way, all of whose officers had been killed or wounded. He had explained exactly what they were to do: in brief, to advance as soon as they saw No 1 Company start to move up the shoulder of the Razorback. He now had to give orders to the Lothians and to No 1 Company, and to co-ordinate the artillery support. He was also able, thanks to the wireless set, to range the guns.

Rhys-Williams had already done more than might be expected of an adjutant. But the companies had had a gruelling time in the heat. They had suffered considerable casualties, only one officer, Lieutenant Stewart, was left standing, and it was, moreover, their first battle. He saw that more was needed than a new plan and additional support from artillery and tanks. That something was leadership, which he proceeded to give in inspired fashion. He got out of his carrier and, ably supported by Stewart, personally led No 1 Company up the hill. The whole way up he encouraged his men by voice and example, and it is without doubt that his spirit gave the urgency which made the final surge up the hill irresistible.

At the top of the hill the leading troops suffered heavily from a shower of grenades lobbed from behind the rocky spine. Still leading, Rhys-Williams leaped over the spine and managed to scatter the bombers before he was killed.

As soon as the other companies saw No 1 move they also started forward. But with the Razorback lost, and the Lothians now shooting across the reverse slope, the Germans withdrew. By mid-afternoon the whole feature and 100 prisoners were in the Battalion's hands. Their own casualties were 9 officers and 105 NCOs and Guardsmen.

Much of the credit for the fine result must go to Rhys-Williams. He had rallied the Battalion at a critical moment and ensured sweeping success in its first action, which in turn made a green battalion battle-worthy and gave them confidence in the future. The regiment owes him a great debt.

1943: 3rd Battalion, North Africa—Hammam Lif

After the 3rd Battalion had taken the high ground over-looking it, the tanks of 6th Armoured Division forced the pass that evening, and two days later the 1st and 8th Armies made contact at Kairouan. Both armies were now under the Command of General Alexander. This gave him the flexibility to group as required, and so maintain maximum pressure on the German and Italian forces. They were now surrounded and the noose was drawn steadily tighter.

On 22 April there was a thrust against the mountains northwest of Pont du Fahs in which 6th Armoured Division took part. But although 1st Guards Brigade was deployed, and the Welsh Guards suffered considerably from shelling and heavy air attack from dive-bombers, they took no direct part in what developed into a tank battle on the Goubellat Plain. The direction of the attack was then switched along the Majerda Valley, aimed directly at Tunis.

The final attack started on 6 May; on the 7th the armoured cars of the 6th Armoured Division were in the outskirts of Tunis; on the following day the Division turned eastward towards the Cap Bon Peninsula. By midday the leading tanks had reached Hammam Lif. Here the mountains of the hinterland sweep down almost directly into the sea, leaving a gap of only about 800 yards. The gap is plugged by the town of Hammam Lif itself. Both town and the hill above, the Djebel el Rorouf, were heavily defended, and the Germans reckoned that it was an almost impregnable position. But it had to be taken quickly to deny the enemy time to organize a stand in Cap Bon. A frontal assault on the town would be a costly enterprise; the tanks could not get through until the Rorouf overlooking it had been taken. This task was given to the Welsh Guards.

When the order was given at about 1330 hours, the Battalion was three miles away on a road choked with tanks, guns and transport of all sorts. It was not until nearly 1500 hours that the attack could start. The companies were able to assemble under cover of some olive groves, which ran more or less parallel to the foot of the hillside. There was then a varying distance of open ground to cover before the Djebel rose steeply to a height of about 750 feet. Along much of the crest, in some places only about two yards wide, ran the same sort of rocky frill which had topped the summit at Fondouk.

The crest was divided into three clearly defined sections, and the Commanding Officer decided to attack the two inland, or right-hand, of these sub-features: 'Double Hill' on the far right and 'Cave Hill' in the centre, and then turn seaward towards 'Little Hill' on the left. At ten to three, in the full heat of the afternoon, the attack started with No 3 Company directed at Double Hill and No 2 at Cave Hill.

Well before the companies advanced, the artillery had been shelling every known enemy position with generous abandon, and this barrage enabled them to cross the open ground beyond the olive groves without too much trouble, and also saw them some of the way up the hill. But as they approached the crest, the barrage had to stop, which allowed the Germans to get their heads up, and their machine gun and mortar fire at once increased in volume and accuracy at close range. In spite of this No 3 Company pressed on, slipping and cursing on the loose surface, until the leading platoon, under Lieutenant O. N. M. H. Smyth, got close enough to assault a German post, which surrendered with 13 prisoners. It seemed as if things were going well.

But it turned out that the position was even stronger than it looked. The Djebel lay back in a slight crescent, so that Little Hill at the seaward end covered the rear of the other two features. Any attempt to cross the rocky spine drew heavy casualties.

On the left No 2 Company had also come under heavy fire. Their approach had been very exposed and although some of them managed to fight their way on to the crest, they were too weakened by casualties to be able to clear Cave Hill. On this occasion the wireless sets were working well. Without delay the Commanding Officer was able to put in his reserve companies, supported across the open ground by the Lothians and the artillery, who ranged further back on to Little Hill. It was now five o'clock and a little cooler.

On the left Major Dimsdale took No 1 Company up a gully, and then keeping well below the crest assaulted and captured Cave Hill. As it was getting dark, he was ordered to stand fast and consolidate for the night.

Meanwhile Major Gibson-Watt, with No 4 Company, had got up Double Hill without difficulty and rushed the crest with one platoon (Lieutenant D. F. Pugh), which then dropped into some thick scrub on the far side. The Company then turned left and worked their way along the hill, with Pugh tearing his way through the scrub, and another platoon, under Sergeant T. H. Evans, working along the ridge. They then reached an open strip where the scrub had been cleared from top to bottom of the back of the hill. It was impossible to cross without attracting heavy mortar and machine gun fire. Gibson-Watt therefore led his reserve platoon, under Sergeant Nelson Rees, down to the bottom of the hill under cover of the scrub. At the bottom they found a gulley which led to a cement factory on the outskirts of Hammam Lif. Entrenched by the factory was the mortar which had caused them so much trouble at the top of the hill. By creeping along the gully they were able to assault without warning, and the startled Germans fled. Leaving Sergeant Rees with his foot in the back door of Hammam Lif, Gibson-Watt returned to the rest of his company on the hilltop, where he too got the order to consolidate for the night.

At dusk the firing died down. The strength of the position had been broken, and when the Coldstream moved through the Welsh Guards during the night, they cleared the rest of the ridge with little opposition.

At dawn the next day the armour resumed its attack on Hammam Lif, no longer overlooked by the enemy. It was during this attack that the Lothian and Border Horse, who supported the Welsh Guards throughout North Africa and Italy, drove their tanks through the sea in a dashing movement which outflanked, and then broke, the last organized enemy resistance on this front.

On the 11th the Battalion entered Nabeul on the east coast of the Cap Bon. There they received their first welcome from a liberated town, and were greeted with wine and flowers by an almost delirious population. They had considerable difficulty in controlling the junketing mob, and at the same time dealing with the prisoners who began to flood in. The Italian soldiers were as happy as the townsfolk; the Germans were sullen, but nevertheless wired themselves into prisoner-of-war cages with speed and efficiency. The Battalion channelled 3,000 prisoners through their hands that day; the final total resulting from General Alexander's great victory was 267,000.

The cease-fire was finally broadcast at five o'clock the next afternoon, when the last German division to resist fired its remaining two shots, one at the 1st and the other at the 8th Army. It was appropriate that the first troops of the 8th Army that the Battalion met were 201st Guards Brigade. A noteworthy celebration followed.

5 THE SECOND WORLD WAR: 1944

3rd Battalion: Italy—Cerasola

The defeat of the German and Italian armies in North Africa had been complete. But for most of the Allied armies there had been little respite. Two months later, on 10 July, British and American forces had landed in Sicily; and on 9 September they had landed on the mainland of Italy at Salerno.

The 6th Armoured Division, in which the Battalion continued to serve, was not to be required until January 1944. They therefore had seven months in which to retrain, refit, absorb reinforcements and to enjoy such facilities for leave and relaxation as there were. They remained on the coast, at Sousse, until August, where there was bathing and basking in the Mediterranean sea and sun, if nothing else. In August they were moved to Constantine, in Algeria, 1,000 feet above sea level, and when Christmas came there was by contrast snow, which gave a seasonable touch to the usual festivities. These included an hilarious and remarkably crooked race meeting at the local course. But at the end of January they were called for, and on 5 February they landed at Naples. They went almost straight into action.

By January 1944 General Alexander had conquered about a third of the Italian peninsula, up to a line about 110 miles south of Rome. The Allies had also landed at Anzio, some 90 miles behind the main front. The aim was for the main forces to join up with the landing. But the Germans had managed to contain the assault at Anzio; they had also established a skilfully chosen line of defence across Italy, dominated by mountains or guarded by rivers.

Four days after disembarking at Naples the Battalion was pitch-forked into harsh and confused fighting on Monte Cerasola, behind the river Garigliano. Cerasola stands 1,000 feet above sea level, and for ten days the Welsh Guards had to contend, not only with continuous fire, but with snow, sleet and freezing rain. A curtain of rock ran along the top of the mountain, the opposing positions on either side of it often being only a few yards apart. It was impossible to dig, and cover could only be achieved by building sangars of loose rock.

As they moved up into this uninviting position, the Commanding Officer, Lieutenant-Colonel Sir William Makins, and his 'O' Group were attacked during the preliminary reconnaissance. But somehow, in snow and darkness, and in spite of almost continuous attack during the night, the companies managed to establish themselves. There were further attacks at dawn, which the Battalion beat off with grenade and bayonet from positions they had not yet seen by daylight. They then found that they were hanging on to the rim of a basin, and that many of the platoons were without adequate cover. They had taken over from the gallant 5th Hampshires, who were badly under strength, so that their sangars were too few and too small for Guardsmen. That first day was spent strengthening their defences.

The dawn attacks (there were two of them) had been pressed home with the greatest of determination by the Germans, the brunt falling on No 2 Company. Twice the enemy reached the crest, twice they were driven off at the point of the bayonet. On each occasion the officer leading the charge was killed; first Captain D. P. G. Elliot, the Company Commander, and then Lieutenant R. G. Barbour who took over from him.

There were no further attacks that day. But No 2 Company was reduced to only 38 men, and altogether 22 were killed and 49 wounded. This at once presented the Battalion with one of the first problems of mountain warfare: the acute difficulty of evacuating a wounded man, especially in winter, down steep, narrow and rocky paths—or no paths at all. At Cerasola, for instance, it took relays of six stretcher-bearers up to 36 hours, and never less than 12, to carry a wounded man down to base. It was only the devoted efforts of the Battalion's Medical Officer, Captain O. D. Morris, and his staff that time and time again such journeys were made tolerable.

Conversely there was the problem of bringing up ammunition, rations and even water, of which there was none on Cerasola except rain or melted snow. The Battalion shaved once, after which, unusually for Guardsmen, the men were encouraged to grow beards.

Later in the campaign a routine was developed which made supply in the mountains a smoother operation. But when the Battalion arrived on Cerasola, only hurried arrangements had been made, which involved bringing stores as far as the river by jeep, ferrying them across, loading them on to mules, with a final carry on the backs of East African porters. But the Quartermaster, Captain K. W. Grant, never failed; boots, ammunition, rations and mail arrived and were distributed every night.

After the first day the Battalion adjusted to its harsh surroundings. But although everything possible was done to alleviate the bitter conditions, frostbite and exhaustion took as steady a toll as mortar and shellfire. A number had to be evacuated sick, including the Commanding Officer, who was very ill, but stuck it out until he was ordered away by the Brigade Commander. But in circumstances such as these, which are not uncommon in war, more than fortitude against the elements is required. Aggressive patrolling must be maintained, to gain information, to act as eyes and ears beyond the immediate limits of forward positions, to harass the enemy, and to make it uncomfortable for his own patrols engaged in similar ventures. Under the determined command of Major D. G. Davies-Scourfield, this sort of pressure was kept up.

Before dawn on 19 February, the day the Battalion was due to be relieved, the Germans made a last attempt to recapture Cerasola. Preceded by a heavy mortar and artillery barrage, they made a frontal assault on the position. This turned out to be a diversion. The real attack came on the right, or northern flank, over an easier slope which led into the centre of the Battalion position, so that the companies found themselves being attacked from the rear. Even Battalion Headquarters was engaged.

Although this was a tricky situation, it was not so dangerous as it appeared. As dawn broke and the light grew stronger, it was the Germans who were at a disadvantage. The companies had held their positions on the rim of the mountain. From the inside ring of the crescent they were able to pour a withering fire on to the Germans, now below them.

A second enemy force also tried to get between the left of the Battalion and the Coldstream Guards, on the neighbouring mountain of Ornito. But they chose an open approach and found themselves exposed on a killing-ground of which the Coldstream made good use. The Germans were caught. Many were killed and the rest surrendered, and by the end of the morning the 3rd Battalion had captured 112 prisoners.

That night a tired, bearded, but triumphant Battalion wound its way down the mountainside. The last in the long file on the narrow track was Major Davies-Scourfield, a badly poisoned foot swathed in a sandbag because he could no longer get a boot on.

3rd Battalion: Italy—Cassino

After a well-deserved rest the Battalion returned to the line on St David's Day, to Monte Purgatorio, an easier slope to the right of Cerasola. Here they were not in close contact with the enemy, but they held a wide front of about 4,000 yards, which demanded intensive patrolling. There was some shelling and mortar fire, but casualties were mercifully fewer than they had been on Cerasola. But if nothing of note happened on their own front, on 15 March, eight miles away across the Liri Valley, the Allies made their third attempt to capture the town and monastery of Cassino.

The town of Cassino lies on the Rapido River, just before it flows into the Liri and then on into the Garigliano. The valley with its road (Route 6) and railway provides the main access to Rome from the south. Looming above all, valley, road and town, is the great Benedictine monastery and the hill, 1,700 feet high, on which it is built. It is an unrivalled strategic position of great strength, with uninterrupted views over all approaches.

Three times the Allies had attempted to capture it: on 17 January in conjunction with the landing at Anzio; on 15 February when the monastery had been bombed; and on 15 March when the town was reduced to rubble by 500 bombers and 620 pieces of artillery. The great column of black smoke which towered into the air was easily seen from Purgatorio. On this occasion the attack was partially successful in that about half the town and Castle Hill were taken by the New Zealanders.

On 7 April, after holding ground to the south of the town for a week, the Battalion moved into Cassino itself, taking over from a New Zealand battalion. During the weeks they were to spend there, the Battalion were neither attacked nor themselves made an attack. But no Welsh Guardsman who served in Cassino will ever forget the place, or the strange underground, nocturnal existence they led there. They even had to talk in low voices to avoid giving away their exact positions to the enemy only the width of a narrow street away.

Entry into the town was in itself a weird business. The

ground was flooded, partly because the bombing had destroyed the banks of the Rapido and partly because the Germans had blown the dam higher up the valley. The marshy swamp gave off a swirling mist, and from the sullen waters thousands of bull-frogs lent their harsh voices to the chill night air. On the shoulder of Monastery Hill stood the gaunt apparatus of the old rope railway; on a moonlit night it had all the appearance of a gallows. In strange counter-point to the shell and mortar fire, and the occasional burst of a machine gun, nightingales sang with abandon. ('We must', said the Commanding Officer who got lost one night, 'be in Berkeley Square.') Beneath the canopy of song were dozens of putrefying corpses, American, Indian and New Zealanders, who had taken part in the three fruitless attacks.

From the edge of the town the route was taped to the various positions. Battalion Headquarters was in a small room, perhaps a cell, in what had been the town gaol. Into this claustrophobic space were crammed the Commanding Officer and his staff. Dimly lit by a lamp or two, at night the small window was covered with blankets to keep in even this small gleam, and at the door hung two sets of blankets to form a light trap. Beyond lay the platoon and section positions, usually in cellars with the ruins of a house heaped on top.

All activity—reliefs, ration parties tumbling in over the rubble, or strengthening positions—had to take place at night, under cover of a smoke-screen which thickened up the river mist. And by both day and night a close, tense watch had to be kept on the enemy; any movement was immediately answered by fire. The mortars especially were swift to respond to any call on a variety of targets corresponding to code numbers on marked air photographs.

So close to the enemy were many of the positions that it seemed possible that, not only were wireless messages being intercepted, but that even telephones could be tapped. The Signals Officer therefore arranged for all messages to be passed in Welsh. His judgement proved to be right: a day or two later the Battalion was showered with propaganda pamphlets—in Urdu.

The Battalion's first stint in Cassino ended on 24 April. On 5 May they returned. On this second tour the castle was added to their responsibilities. The castle lay on a subsidiary spur which juts out from the main mass of Monastery Hill, and is about 450 feet high. It had been taken in the third attack, and although completely dominated by the mountain above it, it in turn dominated the northern half of the town and had to be held. The worst part was getting into position, a stiff half-hour climb carrying rations and ammunition, only made possible by the aid of ropes stapled to the side of the mountain. The Allies own smoke shells often fell unpleasantly close and made breathing difficult; and the stench of decomposing bodies on the way up, and in the castle itself, made it a sickening journey. When the town fell and the castle garrison emerged into daylight, they counted 74 bodies, of different nationalities, up to and around the position—grim testimony of the ferocious fighting that had taken place there.

On 11 May the final battle for Cassino started. It was part of a general advance. Far to the left the Americans pushed up the coast; the French, from the positions which the Battalion had held on Cerasola, made good headway through the mountains; to the left of Cassino the British launched an assault across the Rapido and up the Liri Valley. On the right the Polish Corps attacked over the mountains above the town.

It was here that perhaps the fighting was at its most bitter. The Poles had many memories of the German invasion of their country, and many scores to pay off; the Germans could expect no quarter. In the rough, rocky country the fighting became a bloody hand-to-hand affair. A Polish liaison officer, who had been attached to Brigade Headquarters, at one point reported that a number of prisoners had been taken and would be passing through to the cage prepared for them.

After some hours had elapsed the officer was asked where the prisoners were. He went to his wireless set to check. He returned looking slightly guilty. 'I am afraid,' he said, 'that they have been lost.'

At last, on 18 May, the town fell, pinched out on both sides. The Battalion emerged, blinking into the bright sun, to see for the first time in daylight the positions they had held for a total of 29 days. The battle rolled away up the Liri Valley; outside the door of the gaol a single and beautiful rose grew out of the rubble.

3rd Battalion: Italy—Piccolo and Arce

The fall of Cassino compelled the Germans to retreat, which they did most skilfully. The Allies, who had also broken out of the Anzio beachhead, were now advancing on all fronts, and by the end of June, although there was to be some hard fighting on the way, were to have driven the Germans back for a distance of about 200 miles.

After leaving Cassino the Welsh Guards and the other battalions of 1st Guards Brigade rejoined 6th Armoured Division, and followed the line of battle as it rolled up towards Rome. On 24 May the Division passed through the Adolf Hitler Line, where it had been breached by the Canadians, with orders to lead the advance.

On the morning of the 26th the tanks were held up about five miles short of Arce, which lies across the main road and the junction of another which branches off into the mountains, and which would provide the Germans with another escape route if not quickly captured. The Welsh Guards were well back in the column when they were ordered to come forward, riding on the backs of the tanks of the Lothian and Border Horse. It was some time before they could make their way up over a road choked with all the paraphernalia of an advancing army.

During the afternoon the Battalion eventually reached an assembly area about six miles from Arce and a little later the Commanding Officer and the company commanders were able to make a rather limited reconnaissance from behind the Grenadier lines. But it was plain from the map that two miles in front of the town Route 6 passed through a narrow defile, with Monte Orio on the right, and on the left Monte Piccolo and Monte Grande. It was 11 p.m. and a dark night when the Battalion left the assembly area; their objective was the high ground beyond Arce.

Intelligence reports had indicated that the enemy was evacuating Arce and was not holding the hills in front of it. But as the Battalion slogged along there was some intermittent shelling, not enough to delay them, but enough to arouse the suspicions of the Commanding Officer. With the hills looming closer he decided that he could go no further into the jaws of the pass until he had some definite indication of the enemy's intentions. Accordingly he halted the Battalion and ordered the companies to take up positions astride the road and wait until dawn.

The wisdom of his decision was soon proved. At first light, when supporting arms moved up, it was clear from some very accurate shelling that the enemy had, at the least, a number of observation posts on the high ground, and that the heights must be cleared before the advance could continue. No 4 Company (Major J. R. Martin Smith) was ordered to send a fighting patrol on to Monte Orio on the right, and No 2 Company to make a reconnaissance in force on to Piccolo on the left.

The fighting patrol from No 4 Company, 12 men under Lieutenant T. B. Hayley, made apparently good progress towards the summit of the spur of Monte Orio, which overlooked the road. But near the top they were ambushed, and only three eventually returned; the remainder, including Hayley, were all killed or wounded. Major Martin Smith then decided to work his way back to the spur. Most of the day was spent manoeuvring through the foothills and up the face of the mountain, and by nightfall, with the support of tanks for part of the way, the Company was established on the crest of Monte Orio.

Monte Piccolo is a less insignificant feature than its name implies. It is a long, rocky spur at right angles to the road, presenting to the attacking troops a steep face, terraced into steps two to three feet high for olive trees. At the foot of the slope there lay a thick belt of trees. Probing their way through this belt, the leading platoon of No 2 Company veered too far to their left, and because wireless communication had broken down, Major Cobbold went after them to try to get them back on course. But the platoon had already come under heavy fire; several were killed, including Cobbold before he could reach them. Only a few were able to get themselves back that evening.

In the meantime the other two platoons were sweating up through the olive trees, and in spite of casualties had almost reached the top when they came under fire from front and flanks. Lieutenant I. P. Bankier, now in command, managed to silence some of the enemy posts, but his reduced company remained outnumbered, and continued to suffer from the vicious cross-fire. Seeing that he would be unable to take his objective, Bankier ordered Lieutenant J. H. G. Davies to withdraw the remnants of the Company, which he did with great skill, although wounded. Bankier remained behind with five others to cover the withdrawal, fighting until they were all killed.

No 2 Company's attack had revealed not only the enemy's true strength, but his determination to cover Arce for as long as possible. That night, the Battalion shifted back slightly to avoid the heavy shelling to which even the reserve companies had been subjected throughout the day.

The next morning a full brigade operation was put in hand to capture not only Monte Piccolo, but Monte Grande to its left. That night, after comprehensive preparation by the divisional artillery, heavy mortars and shelling by the armoured brigade, Piccolo was attacked by the Coldstream. But as soon as the barrage had ceased, the Germans, who had taken cover behind the ridge, returned to their positions on the crest, and for the rest of the night, and for most of the following day, some very sharp fighting ensued. The Germans still held, in some strength, a position in depth which covered their forward posts, from a spur which jutted out from the main bulk of Piccolo.

At six in the evening, after further artillery preparation, No 1 Company, Welsh Guards, under Major Gibson-Watt, moved through the Coldstream positions to capture this vital spur. The leading platoon, under Sergeant Elfed Morgan, manoeuvred their way forward and captured a rocky outcrop which concealed several machine guns. But the Germans' stubborn defence was only gradually broken. A number of individual acts of gallantry contributed to the final result: Guardsman T. J. L. Arnold twice took command of a group of men, each time making further ground; and Guardsman C. J. Keogh advanced, firing a bren gun from the hip, was twice wounded, twice had the gun blown from his hands, but continued against the nearest post.

However the greatest act of self-sacrifice was that of Lance-Sergeant Frank Goodwin. He was in command of a section whose objective was a machine gun post in a sangar at the top of the hill. Between Goodwin and the machine gun lay 80 yards of open ground, swept not only by the gun to his front but by three others. Goodwin, disregarding the hail of fire, led his section steadily forward, shooting as he went. On reaching the sangar he dropped his gun to throw in grenades. The gun continued to fire and then stopped. When his section reached him, the German gunner was dead; so was Goodwin, his arms thrown round the gun which he had silenced with his own body.

By nightfall the hill was at last in Allied hands, and during the night the enemy withdrew from Arce. The Germans had fought hard, imposing a delay of three days which allowed a correspondingly large number of their forces to escape northwards. The action cost 1st Guards Brigade nearly 300 casualties, of whom 112 were Welsh Guardsmen. Twenty-two of these were from the platoon of which Lance-Sergeant Goodwin's section was part, and of No 2 Company, only 46 remained under Company Sergeant-Major B. F. Hillier.

With Arce fallen the advance could continue, which it did at a great rate—75 miles in the next week—and by the end of June, 6th Armoured Division would have notched up 200 miles since the Fall of Cassino on 18 May.

A week after the fighting at Piccolo, on 5 June, the Battalion swept past Rome, with the dome of St Peter's clearly visible on the horizon. The city itself fell unopposed to the Americans. But as the 3rd Battalion settled down in their bivouacs that night, a great armada slipped away from the dark shores of England and headed for the coast of Normandy.

1st and 2nd Battalions: Return to France

After the formation of the Guards Armoured Division in 1941, the 1st and 2nd Battalions were to train hard for nearly three years before they were able to put their new-found expertise to the test of war. In the early days there had been little equipment, and much of that was obsolete, like the decrepit Covenenter tanks on which the 2nd Battalion first trained before moving on to Crusaders, Centaurs and, finally, the excellent Cromwell, which they took into battle.

There were also frequent changes in organization, which to begin with had been too strongly influenced by the experience of armoured warfare in the desert, and there was too great a preponderance of tanks over infantry. But as the many exercises proved, the closer fighting in northwest Europe demanded an equal proportion of infantry to allow the most intimate infantry/tank co-operation, down to the lowest tactical level. It was not until after battle experience had been gained in Normandy that the ideal grouping was to be found.

It was with growing impatience that the 1st and 2nd Battalions waited for the day when they would return to France. In April they moved south from Yorkshire, where they had put the final edge on their training, to concentration areas in Brighton and Eastbourne. From there, on 6 June, they could see some of the over 5,000 ships, great and small, engaged on the vast and hazardous enterprise of transporting and supporting the Allied armies across the Channel: 5 divisions on that first day, the first instalment of a total that would eventually mount to 5 million men, a million vehicles and 18 million tons of stores.

Although the Guards Armoured Division was not required for the initial assault, their turn was not to be long delayed. From 18 June they started to cross in detachments, landing at the artificial harbour at Arromanches.[1] By the evening of the 26th both battalions were concentrated a little to the east of Bayeux. It was a surprisingly peaceful setting, though the 1st Battalion had little time to enjoy it. On the 28th they took over a quiet sector of the line at Bretteville l'Orgueil-leuse, and the following day, with 32nd Guards Brigade which was detached from the Division, were sent to hold a line behind some newly-won ground which was not yet secure. They took up positions on the reverse slopes, behind the Orne valley, where the British and Canadian forces were fighting their way towards Caen. The 1st Battalion was posted at the little village of Cheux, about eight miles west of Caen. It had been half destroyed by shellfire and the air

---

[1] There were two of these harbours (code-named Mulberry); one supported the British and one the American beaches. They were prefabricated in England and towed across the Channel. They consisted of floating piers attached to caissons which were sunk on arrival. First projected by Churchill in 1917, each harbour was the size of Dover.

was heavy with the sickly-sweet smell of dead cows and horses, a stench which was to lie over many of the subsequent battlefields in the closely farmed countryside of Normandy. They held this position for 12 days, but the fighting in front of them was successful, and they were not called upon to take part. On 11 July they rejoined the armoured Division near Bayeux.

Although during this period they had had no direct contact with the enemy, the fortunes of war did not leave them unscathed. On the very first evening, when Battalion Headquarters was still digging in, it was heavily mortared. A number of Guardsmen were wounded, and so were the Commanding Officer, the Second-in-Command, the Anti-tank Gun and Signals Officers; all had to be evacuated to England. The following evening Major J. E. Fass, who had taken command, was killed in the same way and in almost the same place. Major C. H. R. Heber-Percy was promoted to take command of the Battalion.

When the Allies landed their main forces, early in the morning of 6 June, the objectives were for the Americans on the right to capture Cherbourg, and for the British on the left to capture Caen. When the 1st Battalion went into the line, Cherbourg had been taken the day before, and the bulk of Caen lying to the north of the river Orne was taken on 6 July.

Phase I of the plan thus accomplished, the second phase could now be put into train. This was for the British to threaten to break out from the Caen, or left sector, attracting as much enemy armour as possible while the real break-out was made by the Americans on the right.

Operation Goodwood started on 18 July. A strong force led by three armoured divisions, the 11th, the 7th and the Guards, attacked east of Caen into the Caen Plain, which lies south and east of the town. The objective of the Guards Armoured Division, on the left flank of the thrust, was the high ground just to the south of Caen, and then if all

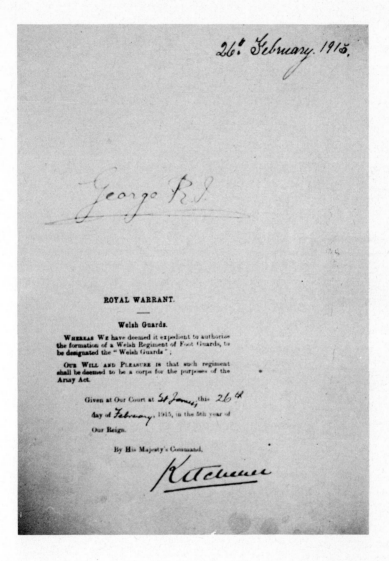

26ᵗ February. 1915.

George R.I.

ROYAL WARRANT.

——

Welsh Guards.

WHEREAS WE have deemed it expedient to authorize
the formation of a Welsh Regiment of Foot Guards, to
be designated the "Welsh Guards";

OUR WILL AND PLEASURE is that such regiment
shall be deemed to be a corps for the purposes of the
Army Act.

Given at Our Court at St. James, this 26ᵗʰ
day of February, 1915, in the 5th year of
Our Reign.

By His Majesty's Command,

Kitchener

1   Royal Warrant, dated 26 February 1915. This appears to be
the only extant official document referring to the formation of
the Regiment

2 First recruiting poster. Subsequent recruiting posters usually show the Colours and the Regimental badge

3　Lieutenant-Colonel W. Murray-Threipland. From a book of cartoons of his brother officers, by Lieutenant P. A. L. Evans

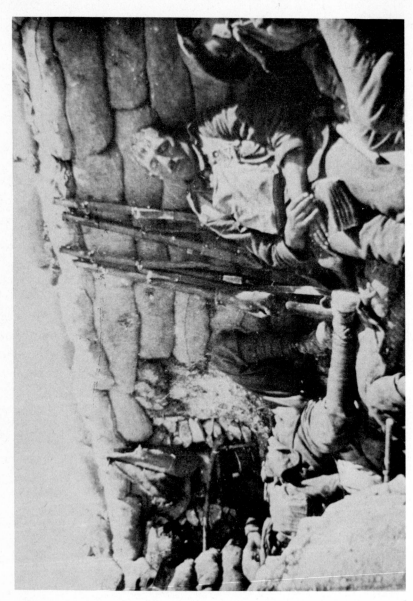

4 Welsh Guardsmen asleep in a trench at Boyelles. This photograph was taken by Captain N. M. Harvey in 1918

5 Sergeant R. Bye, VC, being decorated by King George V

6　Dawn breaking over Dunkirk beaches during withdrawal, June 1940. By Sergeant C. Morrel

7   Lieutenant the Hon. Christopher Furness, VC

8   Portrait of Sergeant J. W. Isaacs, Master Cook of the 2nd
Battalion, by Rex Whistler

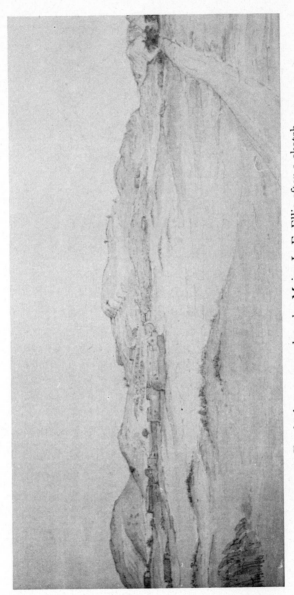

9 Fondouk, a watercolour by Major L. F. Ellis after a sketch by Lieutenant O. N. M. H. Smyth

10   Cassino, by Major L. F. Ellis

11   The road to Brussels, by Sergeant C. Morrel

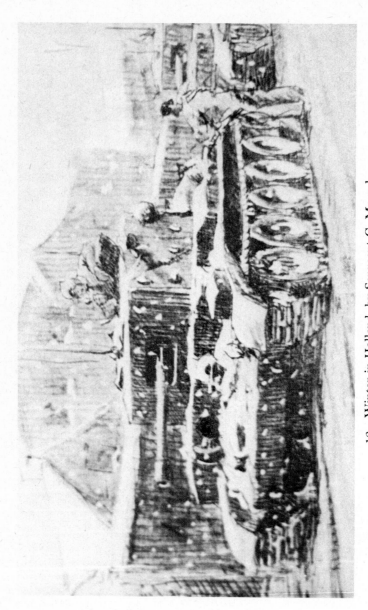

12 Winter in Holland, by Sergeant C. Morrel

13   Welsh Guardsman, 1945, by Augustus John, OM

14   Aden—the Radfan

15 Northern Ireland—Lance-Sergeant Somerset and
Guardsman Bartlett and a patrol of the Drums Platoon at
Forkill, South Armagh

16 HRH The Prince of Wales, Colonel, Welsh Guards, from a portrait by Richard Foster

went well to make for Falaise, about 20 miles further on.

The approach march started on the evening of the 17th, over bulldozed tracks marked with white tape. A couple of hours before first light the Division was lined up on the high ground north of the Orne, ready to cross by the allotted bridges. When dawn broke they had a grandstand view of the bombing attack which preceded their advance. During this colossal operation the Allied air forces laid a carpet of bombs along the axis of advance. After this the heavy bombers and fighter bombers took over, taking off and landing from air strips beside the divisional column. Then massed artillery opened up, wireless silence was broken, and the Division rumbled slowly forward into a choking cloud of dust thrown up by the bombs and shells, and made still thicker by the dust from their own tracks and wheels.

There was much confused fighting that day, but neither the 1st nor the 2nd Battalions were heavily engaged. The brunt of the fighting was borne by the 5th Guards Armoured Brigade. By late afternoon they had reached Cagny where, after they had dealt with the main opposition, the 1st Battalion was sent in to clear the village. After the devastating bombing of the morning the Germans were only too keen to give themselves up, and many prisoners were taken.

The next day, the 19th, the 1st Battalion was ordered to capture Le Poirier, a village three-quarters of a mile south-west of Cagny. Again the opposition was light, and it was taken with little trouble, together with some prisoners. That evening they dug in on the outskirts of the village, where they remained until the 23rd.

Meanwhile the 2nd Battalion had been screening the left flank of the Division. On the first day they had supported a company of the 1st Grenadiers in the capture of Le Prieure Wood, an orchard and some houses. They then moved south a little to cover the ground between Cagny and Emieville, still strongly held by the enemy, where they also remained until the 23rd. During this period both battalions suffered a number of casualties[1] from shell and mortar fire, and the 2nd Battalion lost a number of tanks by mines, anti-tank guns, and through tank-to-tank action.

For the first three days of Goodwood the weather had been glorious. Then the rain fell in sheets and the operation bogged down, in every sense (all of No 7 Troop's tanks were stuck in the mud). The Germans, by good tactics and a little luck, had just managed to hold the British attack. Indeed for those who took part Goodwood seemed a scrappy affair with an indecisive result. And as far as the Guards Armoured Division was concerned, the battle had revealed that there were still weaknesses in organization: armour had out-stripped infantry, which had been unable to intervene at the critical time, and on occasion infantry had been unsupported by armour. For the next battle, although the arrangement remained flexible, 5th Guards Armoured Brigade had the permanent loan of an infantry battalion, and 32nd Guards Brigade took in exchange an armoured battalion.

Nevertheless the battle had achieved its overall object. Six Panzer divisions and all three battalions of Tiger tanks had been attracted against the left, or British, sector of the front, leaving only two Panzer divisions facing the Americans on the right, considerably helping their planned breakthrough which started on 27 July. By the 27th the Americans were moving fast, and on the 28th the weight of the British effort was switched from the Caen sector to Caumont, 25 miles to the west, to support and broaden the American thrust and to protect their now vulnerable left flank.

1st and 2nd Battalions:
Normandy—the Battle of the Breakout

For the next fortnight the Welsh Guards fought through the

[1] One of those killed was Rex Whistler, who was serving with the 2nd Battalion. Then at the height of his career he was one of England's most distinguished young artists.

bocage—a beautiful, green country of small fields, thick hedges, narrow lanes with steep banks and clear winding streams, and dotted about with little stone-built hamlets and farms. This intricate network of small, close country imposed a fragmented form of fighting in which actions were often fought on a company or squadron basis. It is above all defenders' country, and of this the Germans took determined and skilful advantage, operating in small groups of two or three tanks, a handful of infantry, and a couple of mortars. They either infiltrated these groups at night, or left them hidden until the advancing troops had passed, then harrying their flanks and rear. Nearly every field and hedgerow had to be fought for.

On 30 July both battalions moved from Bayeux (from the same fields in which they had first concentrated after landing in France) to St Martin des Besaces. From there on 1 August the 1st Battalion was ordered to clear the village of St Denis Maisoncelles. They had a hot tiring day of it, working through the thick country, but there was little opposition; by evening they had taken the village, and a patrol had made contact with the Americans on their right.

The following day the Division continued its advance, the main axis being the Caumont–Vire road. First to move was the 2nd Battalion, acting in their proper role of Armoured Reconnaissance Battalion. The Division's right flank was protected by the Americans' advance, but the left flank was exposed to the enemy, still holding tenaciously to their positions in the maze of lanes and hedgerows. The 2nd Battalion was therefore given three tasks on the Division's left: No 2 Squadron, under Major J. O. Spencer, was to reconnoitre the Catheolles–Montamy road; No 1 Squadron, under Major A. A. Bushell, was to reconnoitre from Catheolles towards Montcharivel; No 3 Squadron, under Major W. L. Consett, had the more ambitious task of pushing through St Charles de Percy to the high ground overlooking Estry about ten miles to the southeast.

Spencer and Bushell both probed towards their objectives, both found them firmly held, and were ordered to screen them until they could be dealt with by the following infantry. They were then to continue south in support of No 3 Squadron towards Estry.

Meanwhile No 3 Squadron, with great skill and with slightly easier country to contend with, had made good progress towards Estry. They had found that Courteuil and Montchamp were held; but Consett by-passed both and pushed on, disregarding the threat to his flanks and to his lines of communication, and in the afternoon had arrived at the high ground south of La Marvindiere. Patrolling forward from there, he found that Estry was strongly held, so he deployed on the ridge, where he was later joined by the other two squadrons. They remained there, unsupported by infantry, for the next 48 hours. By day they carried out a programme of aggressive patrolling; by night they were subject to guerrilla-like attacks by small bodies of infantry armed with bazookas, and a number of tanks were lost in this way. There was also the difficulty of getting up supplies. The enemy was liable to be found anywhere up to five miles behind the squadrons, and the nightly supply column had an adventurous time of it, often with a skirmish or two on the way up and another on the way back.

During this battle the battalions fought separately. While the 2nd Battalion was making their dash for and holding the high ground near Estry, the 1st Battalion was fighting its way forward, step by step, towards another ridge, over-looking the Vire–Vassey road. Within ten days, and ten miles as the crow flies, the Battalion or one or more of the companies fought four separate, identifiable, battles. The confused and confusing fighting is reflected in the work of the RAP of the 2nd Battalion on 3 August, when the Medical Officer dealt with 68 casualties from eight different units in one period of three hours.

The first action involved Prince of Wales Company, under

Major J. M. Miller. On 2 August the Battalion was embussed at St Denis Maisoncelles, waiting to move forward. At midday Prince of Wales Company was ordered to secure the high ground, at point 205, on the road to Montamy. On the way Miller had to clear the wood and village of St Pierre Tarentain. This proved easy enough: the wood was already clear of enemy and the village was occupied by some friendly Grenadiers.

The next step was to secure a road junction about 1,000 yards from point 205. This was successfully done, but not before several casualties were suffered from enemy shelling as they were forming up in the village. Once on the road, Sergeant A. A. Seamark led No 3 Platoon along the left-hand hedgerow, pinpointed some enemy short of the objective, and while he held them by fire No 2 Platoon, under Lieutenant D. A. Rogers, made a quick attack from further round on the left and surprised the Germans, who fled. But the Company was now in a dangerously exposed position. Some locals confirmed that Montamy was strongly held; enemy tanks could be heard grinding about in front of them, and heavy machine gun fire was coming from their right flank. It was without regret that they received orders to withdraw and rejoin the rest of the Battalion at Le Pont d'Eloy.

The 1st Battalion remained at Pont d'Eloy for 48 hours. It was clear that the enemy lurked closely around them: a water-truck that took a wrong turning immediately found itself facing a German machine gun post. In this battle it was difficult, if not impossible, to guarantee that any stretch of country had been cleared of enemy.

On the afternoon of the following day the Battalion was put temporarily under command of 44 Brigade, of 15th Scottish Division. The Brigade had orders to attack eastwards along the ridge which runs north of Montchamp, with the Welsh Guards on the right flank. Their first objective was to clear the wood at Courtacon, and after a preliminary barrage they achieved this without much trouble. Nos 3 and 4 Companies then went on to capture Les Fieffes, where a macabre incident took place. A British 3-ton truck drove into No 3 Company's lines from the direction of the enemy. On the roof of the cabin was a German with his hands up, as if in surrender. At point blank range the truck stopped, the cover was pulled back, and a squad of Germans opened up with sub-machine guns. They and the men inside the cabin were killed instantly by the Guardsmen. But the man on the cabin roof, riddled with bullets, his face a ghastly colour, broke into a dirge-like song, chanting, swaying and smiling at the surrounding Guardsmen. When one of them pushed a rifle towards him, he shook his head and continued his death-song among the flames of the now blazing truck, until at last he died.

Later that day the Battalion was ordered to take Montchamp itself, and a dour and confusing battle was to follow. As a first step the Commanding Officer decided to secure his left flank by capturing Pont Esnaut, which commands the road running east of Montchamp. This phase was achieved by Nos 3 and 4 Companies without much difficulty and many prisoners were taken. Half an hour later, at 6 p.m., Prince of Wales and 2 Companies moved in against Montchamp. No 2, on the right, were to take the western half of the village, and Prince of Wales Company, on the left, the eastern half.

As they left their slit-trenches, and before they reached their start-line, Prince of Wales suffered 17 casualties from an enemy artillery concentration; but they had to push straight on, or they would have lost the benefit of their own artillery support. As they made their way through the fields and up the hedgerows towards Montchamp, they came across two tanks, a Mark IV covered by a Panther. Captain Sir Richard Powell crawled forward with a PIAT, let fly at only a few yards range and blasted a hole in the side of the Mark IV, whereupon the Panther hurriedly withdrew. The Company followed behind it into Montchamp, where both they and No 2 Company dealt with a number of snipers, indulged in some brief street-fighting and drove the Germans out of the far side of the village. They started to consolidate, but neither the tanks which were to support them nor their own anti-tank guns were able to arrive before a heavy counter-attack by tanks and infantry bounced back at them.

On the right No 2 Company was cut in half by the tanks, the first of which killed the Company Commander. The left half of the Company managed to withdraw into the village; the right half hung on in their positions until they were ordered to withdraw to a reorganized position which was later established north of the village. Prince of Wales were even harder hit, being completely overrun. With the tanks in amongst them it was impossible to carry out the order to withdraw in an orderly fashion. But Lieutenant D. A. Rogers managed to extricate about 20 men, and most of the others got away in small groups. Miller and Powell were out in front when the attack started. Powell managed to get a hand grenade in among the crew of the nearest tank. Miller, who waited until last to try to control the withdrawal, took a wounded man with him. Powell was less lucky; he was also looking after a wounded Guardsman, but came face to face with a tank. The Guardsman was killed and Powell was knocked unconscious and taken prisoner.[1]

Just before the counter-attack began, the Commanding Officer was wounded by a sniper in civilian clothes, who was caught and shot. Major G. G. Fowke then took temporary command of the Battalion, and when reports of the situation came in he ordered Prince of Wales and No 2 Companies to consolidate a position north of the village. And getting further news that No 4 Company at Pont Esnaut was also being steadily surrounded, he ordered them to conform. By nightfall the Battalion had been reorganized in a strong position with proper support from artillery and tanks.

[1] He later escaped, returning to the Battalion a few weeks later, via Paris, in a German staff car.

For an hour the Battalion had been in a tricky, even a potentially disastrous, position; the German counter-attack had caught them at the fleeting, but always vulnerable, moment of reorganization after an attack. But good leadership and stout fighting had saved the day. The Germans had inflicted over 100 casualties, receiving more in return, and during the night they crept away from Montchamp.

Five days later the Battalion moved south, to take over from the 1st Battalion, the Herefordshire Regiment, round Le Bas Perrier. The position was an uncomfortable one with to their front Le Haut Perrier and on their left flank Houssemagne on a long north–south ridge, which trailed back behind them, all occupied by the enemy.

Lieutenant-Colonel J. F. Gresham, now commanding the Battalion, gave Le Haut Perrier to Nos 2 and 3 Companies and Houssemagne to Prince of Wales and No 4. For once they had plenty of time to make their preparations and to co-ordinate their attack with their supporting armour, the 3rd Battalion, Scots Guards, from 6th Guards Armoured Brigade,[1] and 1st Battalion, Irish Guards, from 5th Guards Armoured Brigade.

The attack on Le Haut Perrier started at 6.30 a.m. on 11 August. No 2 Company reached their objective, a ridge to the left of the hamlet, without much opposition. But No 3 Company, under Lieutenant P. R. Leuchars, had to fight every inch of the way through the thick country. Le Haut Perrier stands on the highest ground in the area, guarding a road running north–south to the main Vire–Vassey road, which the Germans had to keep open as their line of retreat. They used a minimum of infantry, but they adopted the tactics of holding ground with fire from a number of mutually supporting machine gun posts. There were nine such posts defending Le Haut Perrier, supported by three Panther tanks,

---

[1] 6th Guards Armoured Brigade was not part of the Guards Armoured Division, but an independent brigade, soon to be commanded by Brigadier W. D. C. Greenacre, who had trained the 2nd Battalion in its armoured role.

a mortar and some well observed artillery and mortar support—of which full evidence was soon given. The Company suffered 20 casualties from a heavy concentration of mortars as they formed up for the attack.

No 7 Platoon advanced across two fields and silenced a machine gun post before they were held up by further posts away to their right. To go after these posts would divert the attack too far away from its proper objective, Le Haut Perrier, so Leuchars decided to go left-handed. No 7 Platoon thus slipped along the hedge on the left of the road and occupied a sunken lane which ran across their front, about 200 yards from the village. No 8 Platoon, which had gone further left, had reached the outskirts of the village and silenced one machine gun post, when two more opened up on them. A Scots Guards tank which was supporting them, blew up on a mine, but the crew escaped and continued fighting as infantry.

Meanwhile Lieutenant D. J. C. Stevenson, with five men from No 7 Platoon, had crept forward into the village, silenced another machine gun post and killed a couple of snipers. Just after they got back to the sunken road the enemy put down a thick smoke-screen which proved to be signal for their withdrawal. For the moment nothing could be seen by the infantry, but the Scots Guards tanks, more to the flank, spotted and knocked out three Panthers. When the smoke lifted the Company moved into the village. There was now little opposition and they killed several Germans and took a few prisoners. There was one more incident before the village was finally theirs. No 8 Platoon, which had occupied the far end of the village, saw another Panther advancing towards them; the third shot from their PIAT hit fair and square, and the tank burst into flames. One member of the crew escaped, but no one was in the mood for taking prisoners and he was shot.

The village, which had been so peaceful only a few hours before, was now a shambles. There were several burning tanks, three bagged by the Scots Guards. One tank, with a neat hole in its side, still had its engine running and its wireless set still crackling out messages to an unlistening crew.

Half an hour after Nos 2 and 3 Companies had started their attack on Le Haut Perrier, Prince of Wales and 4 Companies moved on Houssemagne. Prince of Wales on Houssemagne itself and No 4 on to the ridge running north from it. Houssemagne was a stiff task for Prince of Wales, which had been reduced by the battle at Montchamp to a strength of only 65. They knocked out two machine gun posts on their way, but on reaching the outskirts of the village they met more machine guns and an anti-tank gun. At one stage the Company attacked some buildings across an open field, but the opposition was strong enough for Major Miller to order a temporary withdrawal to a sunken lane. Eventually, with tremendous support from tanks of the Irish Guards, they managed to consolidate south of the village. But clearing the village was difficult and costly. The Irish Guards lost six of their tanks, and Prince of Wales suffered 30 casualties out of its already small numbers.

During the withdrawal to the sunken lane, the Company clerk, Lance-Corporal F. W. Dyke, noticed that Guardsman Rodgers, the Company storeman, was missing. Dyke ran back to the buildings, and a few minutes later Company clerk reappeared under a hail of bullets, trundling Company storeman to safety in a wheelbarrow.

Meanwhile No 4 Company, under Major W. D. D. Evans, had been heavily shelled as they started off. But with excellent support from the tanks of the Scots Guards and the guns of the Leicestershire Yeomanry, they knocked enemy machine gun posts out of the hedges and ditches, one by one, until they gained their objective on the ridge, another of the sunken lanes that criss-cross the *bocage*. Once there they beat off with grenades a counter-attack by a party of infantry who had crept up through a field of standing corn.

Prince of Wales and No 4 Companies remained in the Houssemagne area until that evening when, relieved by another brigade, they moved south to help Nos 2 and 3 Companies to consolidate the high ground between Le Haut Perrier and Chennedolle.

1st and 2nd Battalions: the Race for Brussels

After the Normandy battles the Division was rested. The fighting had been hard and casualties heavy. In the case of the 1st Battalion, losses could not be made good, and No 2 Company had to be disbanded. Its place was taken by X Company, Scots Guards, under Major P. Steuart-Fotheringham. They served gallantly with the Battalion until, seven months later, further accumulated casualties caused it to be sent home.

Other changes were also soon to take place, and the Division was to assume its final organization. Four regimental battle-groups, Grenadier, Coldstream, Irish and Welsh, each of a battalion of tanks and a battalion of infantry, were formed, to be allotted to the 5th or 32nd Guards Brigades as required. The marriage between the 1st and 2nd Battalions was willingly solemnized at Douai on 2 September, the day before the leap forward to Brussels.

Meanwhile the last stages of the Normandy battle reached a crescendo at Falaise, where the bulk of the German army west of the Seine, 43 divisions, had been surrounded and destroyed. By 21 August the Germans were in full retreat; on the 25th Paris was entered by French and American forces. The opportunity was now offered, and firmly grasped, for the longest and fastest armoured advance in the history of armoured warfare.

On 23 August the Guards Division moved to Mont Cerisy, unspoiled country with rich farms providing plentiful butter, milk and cheese. On the 28th they moved on to l'Aigle.

While they were moving forward the Divisional Commander flew up to see General Horrocks, commanding XXX Corps, who was itching to unslip all possible armour against a now incoherent German defence. The Division was about 100 miles behind the leading troops, but it was agreed that by hard driving, if necessary at night, it could be north of the Seine by 30 August. This was achieved, and by that evening Beauvais was reached, after by-passing some opposition at Arneuil. On the next day came the tremendous news that the Household Cavalry had captured, intact, a bridge over the Somme at Corbie, which was promptly secured by the Grenadier Battle Group.

At first light the Division was off again, with 2nd Battalion, Welsh Guards, leading. They went at top speed down small roads, or direct across the hedgeless country. Large numbers of prisoners were taken, and by evening they had reached their objective, the high ground beyond Arras. In one exhilarating day they had advanced 40 miles.

The day had been equally satisfactory for the 1st Battalion, who were the first British troops to enter Arras in strength, as they had been the last to leave in 1940. The townspeople, realizing who they were, gave them a delirious welcome.

It was during the race for Brussels that the full meaning of liberation to the occupied countries of Europe became apparent to the impatient British soldiers. Delay on the line of advance came less from the fleeing Germans than from cheering crowds of French and Belgians lining the route in every town and village. Fruit, wine and gifts of every sort were pressed into the hands of the willing Guardsmen, and their tanks and trucks, covered in flowers, looked more like carnival floats than military vehicles. And the Resistance movements, which had fought underground for so many dangerous years, came into the open and gave valuable assistance. They guarded the hordes of prisoners, gave information, marked minefields; and at Corbie it had been the Resistance who had removed demolition charges on the bridge after shooting a party of Germans who tried to detonate them. Much of the credit for the capture of the bridge intact goes to the Resistance.

On the next day the battalions moved forward to Douai, where the planned wedding of the 1st and 2nd Battalions took place, as did the union of the other Regimental Battle Groups. But there was little time for celebration. That evening the Division came under starter's orders for the race to Brussels. 'My intention is to advance and liberate Brussels,' said General Adair; 'and a very good intention, too,' he added.

Speed was essential, and any serious opposition was to be by-passed. The move was to take place on two centre lines, with the new Grenadier Group leading on the left and the Welsh Group leading on the right. The distance for both leading groups was about 80 miles, and considerable excitement was added to an already highly keyed atmosphere by the rivalry between the two groups. It occurred to nobody that Brussels would not be reached by nightfall—the question was, who would get there first?

Punctually at 7 a.m. the armoured cars of the Household Cavalry crossed the start-line at Douai, followed by the Welsh Group at 7.25. The Grenadier Group, delayed by slight opposition, left at 8 a.m. Thereafter the story was much the same on both routes. The Welsh Group met their first opposition when the leading squadron bumped an enemy rearguard at Leuze. The tanks tried to force a way through, but it needed a combined infantry/tank attack to clear the way and allow the advance to continue. The Grenadiers met a similar strongpoint at Pont a Marq. It was now about ten o'clock, the two groups were running neck and neck, competition was becoming keener, and it was at about this time that the general was persuaded to choose a finishing post, a road junction where the two routes met, just within the outskirts of the city.

The Welsh Group were now on the Route Nationale, and

for the next 30 miles both columns raced on unchecked, until the Welsh Group met a second strongpoint at Enghein, where they were again checked for about an hour while the infantry deployed to clear the route. The Welsh tank crews took advantage of the delay to do a little much-needed maintenance to their tanks.

It was after this delay that Lieutenant-Colonel Windsor Lewis, with his brigadier's permission, decided to push on at the maximum speed of his Cromwell tanks, 50 mph, even if this meant that some of them might founder on the way. Even so it seemed that the Grenadiers must win, until having got within ten miles of the city limits, they too were again held up by strong opposition at a road and rail crossing, which caused them to deploy their infantry. The Welsh reply was to see if their tanks could not be urged to 60 mph instead of a mere 50, and they roared, double banked, towards the waiting city. They had one more slight skirmish at Hal, but this hardly delayed them, and at 8 p.m. they passed the winning post, just as the Grenadiers entered the outskirts a few minutes behind them.

The welcome given to the Welsh Guards exceeded anything they had known, even over the last few days. The crowd quite simply went wild with joy, undeterred by the snipers' bullets that still whistled overhead, the sharp exchanges of fire at the Pont Namur and in the Arc des Arts, or the furiously burning Palais de Justice, which the Germans had fired in the hope of destroying Gestapo records.

It had been something of a risk to occupy a large city, in darkness, against an enemy of still unknown strength. But the gamble paid off. The various battalions, squadrons and companies, after getting hopelessly lost in the maze of streets, managed to find and settle down in (if that is the phrase) previously allotted sectors—for the jubilation went on far into the night. The tired but exultant Guardsmen were ruthlessly kissed by all and every inhabitant who could get near enough: pretty girls, not so pretty girls and garlicky old men with beards. And the wine flowed. An enormous quantity was undoubtedly drunk, yet throughout the Division not one case of drunkenness was reported, or of a man being unable to perform his duty, either that night or the following day.

But all festivities must come to an end, and in the cold light of day there was much to be done. Maintenance of tanks and vehicles in particular required attention, and for some there was a quick return to reality after the last few heady days.

At about midday on 4 September a message came from the Belgian Resistance that a large body of Germans at Wavre wished to give themselves up, but to the British Army only. Having recently shot the leader of the Resistance there, the Germans had doubts about their fate if they should fall into Belgian hands. Accordingly a small force, under Major G. G. Fowke, was despatched to supervise the surrender. No 4 Company was supported by detachments from the carrier and anti-tank platoons, and by a troop from No 3 Squadron of the 2nd Battalion.

But Lieutenant V. G. Wallace, who had been sent on ahead to make the preliminary arrangements, was shot at and got an arrogant message from the German Commander that the German Army never surrenders. A strange boast after the events of the last weeks. Wallace hurried back to warn the company. Although strictly speaking Wavre lay outside the divisional boundary and was not their responsibility, the small force decided to attack.

Wavre lies more or less north and south of the River Dyle which cuts it into two roughly equal parts. One platoon, Number 12, under Lieutenant E. Scudamore, and the troop of tanks under Captain F. S. Portal, cleared the near, or northern, side of the town, which after some confused street fighting they achieved, though at the cost of several casualties.

Meanwhile the rest of the Company, under Major Evans, worked along the railway line to a monastery, where they came under heavy fire from a Panther tank. Lance-Corporal H. O. Hughes, who tried to get a shot at it with his PIAT, was killed. But the platoons managed to cross the river at a mill, and by evening had cleared the town, helped by Scudamore who, after clearing his own side of the town, had waded over the river at the southern end of Wavre and worked back towards Evans in an effective pincer movement. At nightfall some American armoured cars arrived; the town was handed over to them, and the detachment returned to Brussels.

In January 1945 a few members of No 4 Company re-visited Wavre, and at the monastery they found that the monks had erected a plaque on the spot where Corporal Hughes had fallen, with a white stone cross inlaid in the cement.

3rd Battalion: Italy—Perugia and San Marco

After the fall of Rome the advance up Italy continued. On 8 June, about 15 miles further on, the leading tanks of 6th Armoured Division were held up by shellfire, and the Welsh Guards were called upon to make a night advance up the left bank of the Tiber, where it winds along beside the main road (Route 4). This was successfully achieved without much opposition, but streams and bridges had been accurately registered by the German artillery and the Battalion suffered several casualties from shell and mortar fire, including the Commanding Officer, Lieutenant-Colonel Davies-Scourfield, who was wounded. Command of the Battalion was taken over by Lieutenant-Colonel J. E. Gurney.

The tanks continued the advance the next day, but were again held up, this time by a blown bridge. There followed another long night advance by both Welsh and Grenadier Guards. After this the tanks again took the lead, and in the next ten days covered 75 miles, bringing them to the hills of Perugia without having to call on the infantry for help.

Perugia stands on the end of a south-running spur which overlooks the valley up which the 6th Armoured Division was approaching. By 18 June all 1st Guards Brigade were deployed before this small, ancient city. Except for the railway station and a few untidy factories, Perugia had changed little over the centuries and remained a zigzag of medieval streets within its own walls.

On 19 June the Grenadiers and Coldstream drove in the outposts in front of the town, though the town itself remained in German hands. On the left 61 Brigade captured the high ground which covers the approaches to Perugia from the west, and that night, under cover of darkness, the Germans withdrew back along the ridge on which Perugia stands, towards San Marco, about two miles away. San Marco now became the Welsh Guards' objective.

Very early the next morning Nos 1 and 2 Companies completed the first part of the operation. No 1 Company, under Captain W. T. C. Fogg-Elliot, occupied the road junction near point 427, and then pushed on to point 425. No 2 Company had meanwhile got into a position to cover the road junction near Ponte d'Oddi. It was still dark, and so far there had been no sign of the enemy.

However at daylight, when Captain B. P. R. Goff led No 3 Company through No 1, the enemy made himself felt and started to shell and mortar the road as soon as they moved forward. As they approached a defile the leading platoon came under heavy machine gun fire as well. Goff put a platoon on either side of the road, and supported by the 16/5th Lancers they worked their way forward. The left was cleared without much difficulty, but on the right Lieutenant P. F. F. Brutton and his platoon had a stiff fight for a lone house on the hillside defended by infantry, machine guns and a tank. The tank was dealt with by the 16/5th, and the house was then assaulted by two parties, one under Brutton and the other under Sergeant O. F. Abrahams from a flank. After some sharp hand-to-hand fighting the house was taken.

In the meantime No 4 Company, under Captain F. L. Egerton, who were to have advanced on No 3 Company's left, were late in arriving. After missing a turning in the outskirts of the town, they found themselves in Perugia's main square, where they were hemmed in by a seething crowd of townsfolk determined to load them with gifts of wine, fruit and flowers. But these attentions were temporarily subdued when a few Germans fired some shots from an upper window. Lieutenant J. T. Jerman rounded them up and captured a machine gun, but then had considerable difficulty in preventing his prisoners being lynched by the Perugians. Eventually No 4 Company managed to extricate themselves from town and people and came up on Goff's left.

Some scattered but hard little actions were fought during the rest of the day as one point after another was forced by the Welshmen, supported by the Lancers. But by four o'clock San Marco was theirs.

The Battalion now lay facing northwest with San Marco and Perugia behind them. In front of them, overlooking the line of advance, rose the hill of Mentione, with a long broken ridge stretching out behind. Italian civilians reported that the Germans had withdrawn from there, and Lieutenant-Colonel Gurney ordered No 4 Company to occupy it.

At six o'clock in the evening Captain Egerton led the Company forward. They reached the foot of the hill without opposition, except for some machine gun fire as they crossed the road. They were well up the hill, using a gully for cover, when they were fired on from a sangar on the crest. They replied with rifles and grenades, and as they neared the sangar, they could see the Germans running away.

The Company dug in for the night, but the position was an exposed one. They had cleared the immediate crest, but the hill ran back for miles in a jumble of rock and oak scrub, providing excellent cover for counter-attack by a large force. Moreover they were too isolated from the Battalion to expect immediate support in any emergency. Indeed at about 1 a.m. they were almost surrounded by rifle and spandau fire from a large raiding party which had crept up through the rough ground. Egerton wisely withdrew a little to take advantage of the cover provided by the crest, but at first light he led the Company back to their previous positions. By daylight these proved to be reasonably strong, and patrols were sent out to sweep the area around the position. One of the patrols found a mysterious dump of British rations, which were more than welcome; supplies were short, and now they had food for at least a day. But it was clear that the enemy was still about in some strength; several attacks had to be beaten off, and Egerton was ordered to withdraw that night.

As darkness fell the enemy could be heard once more trying to surround the position, so Captain Egerton ordered his Company to slip away, section by section, and to re-assemble at the bottom of the hill. They managed to do this so quietly that they were gone before the enemy realized it, and without a shot being fired. Soon after midnight they were back in San Marco, in a large house, eating a hot meal off plates and tablecloths—a simple but real luxury for a rifle company at war.

During their first night on the hill, a small party, led by Major, the Baron de Rutzen, had tried to reach them with rations. On approaching the spot where they supposed the Company to be, they heard voices, and called back quietly. Getting no reply, Major de Rutzen shouted, only to be answered by a hail of rifle and spandau fire. Obviously out-numbered the party dumped the rations and crept discreetly away. The Germans they ran into may have been those who attacked No 4 Company later that night. The rations were certainly those which the Company retrieved so surprisingly the next day.

The following morning a further attempt was made to get through to the Company with rations and ammunition. Major Fogg-Elliot and a party, which included CSM Tremblet of

No 4 Company, set out in a wide arc to avoid the post which de Rutzen had bumped the previous night. They captured a prisoner by a farm building, but were immediately fired on from two sides. Tremblet and Sergeant Essex, who was with him, were both too badly wounded to get away. But Fogg-Elliot managed to return to his Company and at once detailed Lieutenant J. D. S. Nicholl-Carne and his platoon to come back with him, destroy the enemy post and rescue the wounded. But the Germans were now well on the alert; both Fogg-Elliot and Nicholl-Carne were killed under the heavy mortar and machine gun fire which greeted them. Unable to take the post the platoon then withdrew. It was this evidence that No 4 Company were too isolated and cut off from the Battalion that decided the Commanding Officer to order them to withdraw that night. It took a battalion attack by the Grenadiers two days later finally to clear the Mentione hill of the enemy, and by the end of June the enemy were finally cleared from the Perugia area.

3rd Battalion: Italy—From Arezzo to the Gothic Line

After losing Perugia and the hills behind it, the Germans attempted to stand on a line across the calf of Italy, with its centre on Lake Trasimene. They were hustled out of it, and made a more determined effort on a line anchored east and west on Ancone and Leghorn, with a strong buttress at Arezzo in the central mountains.

But Field-Marshal Alexander had no intention of allowing them to settle in these new positions, 50 miles behind which the even stronger Gothic Line was being prepared. On 14 July 6th Armoured Division moved forward, with Arezzo as its objective.

The Battalion meanwhile enjoyed a week's rest on the shores of Trasimene. After seven weeks continuous movement, including two major battles, there was much re-organization and administration to be done. Accumulated casualties had weakened the Battalion to the extent that No 2 Company had to be disbanded and its place temporarily taken by a company of Grenadiers, under Major D. Willis. The Grenadiers were warmly welcomed at the 'Cardiff Arms', a large villa which Lieutenant-Colonel J. E. Gurney had requisitioned, and which in the next few months provided a rest centre for those on short leave from the Battalion.

During the Battalion's respite at Trasimene, much hard fighting had taken place further north. The operation against Arezzo, which is guarded by a six-mile mountain ridge, was opened by the New Zealand Corps, who captured the south-eastern end of it. On 15 July 1st Guards Brigade continued the attack through the New Zealanders; first the Grenadiers started the attack in darkness, followed by the Coldstream, who carried a further sector of the crest. Later the Welsh Guards, under a hot midday sun, sweltered up the blistering hills to take the final objective, twin sentinel peaks which flanked the road to Arezzo. They had some casualties from shellfire, but the enemy, outflanked, had gone. Two days later Ancone and Leghorn also fell. The new German front had been broken.

Just north of Arezzo the River Arno loops in a great U-turn, flowing back northwest to Florence. Up this western valley runs Route 69, with a secondary road winding roughly parallel to it through the foothills. The job of 1st Guards Brigade was to guard this, the right flank of 6th Armoured Division, as it advanced up Route 69. They did so in a series of bounds, the battalions leap-frogging from one firm base to another, from which the enemy was continually prodded by patrols. The Battalion was based in turn at Quarata, Renacci, Torre a Monte and San Ellero.

If one must go to war, the Arno valley that summer was not a bad place to do it. The Battalion was not in continuous contact with the enemy; and when not in the lead they could bathe in the alternately green and yellow waters of the

Arno. They could visit nearby towns, or spend a few days right out of it all at the 'Cardiff Arms'. In the afternoons the local custom of the siesta was adopted. For the moment life was a pleasant contrast to the harsh existence of mountain warfare in the winter, on Cerasola the previous winter, or on Battaglia in the winter to come. From Quarata a party was able to attend the King, on a visit to his forward troops at Arezzo.

On 2 August, when the Battalion was based on Renacci, 2nd Lieutenant S. A. Hall took a daylight patrol out to a hamlet called Pian Di Sico. Some Italians told them that four Germans were resting in an outlying farm. Hall, with five men, decided to stalk and capture them. Just before they reached the building they were fired on from a hidden position; Hall and a Guardsman were killed. But Lance-Corporal Hodgson carried on and with the remaining three Guardsmen rushed the building and captured the four Germans. He then realized that he would not be able to get back in daylight, so he drove the prisoners up into the attic. Later that day a party of enemy came to the house, looking for the prisoners and calling for them by name. Hodgson and his men saw to it that the prisoners kept quiet, and in the darkness of the following night got them safely back to the Battalion.

Two days later the Battalion advanced again and No 2 (Grenadier) Company, with two troops of tanks from the Lothian and Border Horse, captured Torre a Monte, a large villa with good observation of the country ahead. At the same time Allied troops had reached the outskirts of Florence, though it was to be another week before they could force a crossing of the Arno and finally enter the city, which the Germans abandoned. Two days later bitter fighting on the Adriatic forced the Germans back another 20 miles. This loss, coupled with the loss of Florence, compelled a general German withdrawal in the centre, from the hills behind Florence.

After a spell in reserve the Battalion returned to the Torre a Monte area, and on 25 August 4 Company captured Altomena, while No 3 Company captured the Grille feature and went on to liberate the small town of Pelago.

The 3rd Battalion was now at the head of the valley, and on 30 August, with the other battalions of 1st Guards Brigade, they secured the northern slopes of the Prato Magno at Podernuovo. From there the Battalion patrolled to Toschi, where they found some German posts which they pushed off the next day. The Battalion then followed the Germans up the Sieve, repeating the technique followed over the last month: probing, pressing, patrolling.

One such, highly successful, patrol was carried out by Lieutenant R. O. Wrigley and his platoon. After a preliminary reconnaissance, Wrigley led his patrol off just before dawn on 4 September, from the Company position a mile or so north of Toschi. The patrol adopted the now standard formation: Wrigley himself, with a small advance-guard of three, including Lance-Sergeant Pickersgill; the main party of a dozen, under Sergeant F. D. Jones; and finally a rearguard under Lance-Corporal K. Culverhouse.

After daylight came the patrol had to move with great care and skill. At about 10 a.m. Pickersgill saw a German helmet balanced on the trunk of a tree. Easing his way forward he came upon a German in a slit-trench trying to light a cigarette. The German surrendered promptly, his cigarette remaining unlit. Ten yards further on the advance-guard found three more Germans, fast asleep, under a bivouac of branches. They also surrendered without trouble. The main party was now signalled up and they established themselves in the German position. The prisoners were escorted away, after it had been learnt from one of them that there was another post 200 yards away along the ridge. There was good cover available, so Wrigley and Pickersgill set off. Once again they were successful, capturing an idle sentry and the rest of the post who, like their friends, were also asleep. They too were sent back under guard, having given the useful information that their platoon sergeant was soon due back. There was not long to wait; the sergeant ran straight into the trap, unfortunately dropping a bottle of wine he was carrying as he put his hands up. The sergeant, as talkative as his men, disclosed the position of a still further post, under an officer, 300 yards away. Wrigley, this time with Culverhouse, stalked this post too. But on this occasion the enemy were alert, opening fire when they were about 100 yards away. But when the fire was returned, the enemy ran away down the hillside.

As Wrigley and Culverhouse returned to the main body, it was attacked by a party of Germans who had come to investigate, and Wrigley ordered his patrol to withdraw. He remained with a small covering party, and just before he too pulled out, he let off the coloured smoke-grenades, which by previous arrangement brought down artillery fire on the spot four minutes after he left it. Wrigley and his platoon were back by 1 p.m. They had captured ten men and their weapons, including two spandaus, without casualties to themselves.

Ten days later the Battalion got their first glimpse of the Gothic Line. But probing forward from Dicomana to Bavello and Villore, they found the wired and concreted positions deserted. The Germans, unable to man them, had drawn back to the higher slopes, and on 16 September, when a patrol climbed the 4,000 feet of Monte Peschiena, it found the Germans there in strength. 1st Guards Brigade was suddenly withdrawn, and after a circular journey via Arezzo found themselves on the slopes of Monte Penna, east of Bibbiena, facing another sector of the Gothic Line. But here too the enemy was withdrawing. A patrol to the top of Monte Vescovi discovered it abandoned.

Meanwhile the Allies were fighting their way ridge by ridge, through the mountains north of Florence. In particular the Americans were waging a bitter struggle up the Santerno valley towards Imola, and on to the commanding feature of

Monte Battaglia, which the Germans were determined to regain. Several counter-attacks had been put in when the Battalion arrived there on 2 October.

1st and 2nd Battalions: Belgium—the Road to Arnhem

The lightning advance of the Guards Armoured Division to Brussels had not been unmatched elsewhere. The 11th Armoured Division took Antwerp on the following day, and on the 5th Ghent fell to the 7th Armoured Division. And the Americans had reached the general line Namur–Tirelemont, so protecting the Division's right flank.

It was now Field-Marshal Montgomery's intention to establish a bridgehead over the lower reaches of the Rhine before winter set in. As their part in the first step in this plan, Guards Armoured Division was to establish itself in the Eindhoven area of Holland; this involved crossing two major waterways, the Albert and the Escaut Canals.

After the great events of 3 September, the Division remained in and around Brussels for two days, the 1st Battalion on the outskirts, and the 2nd Battalion at an exclusive golf club at Quatre-bras, on the old road that saw Napoleon march to his defeat at Waterloo.

At a conference on the evening of the 5th, when the tented divisional headquarters went up in flames due to an over-turned paraffin lamp, the Welsh Guards Group was directed to advance via Diest to Beeringen, which lies astride the Albert Canal, and then on through Helchteren and Hechtel towards the Escaut Canal.

As they drove on from Brussels, with No 3 Squadron and Prince of Wales Company leading, the Welsh Guards Group found Louvain and Deist *en fête*, and it was not until they reached Beeringen that they were fired on. They also found that the bridge, the only one over the canal, had been blown, but only partially destroyed. Lieutenant A. F. Q. Shuldham tried to get his platoon across in single file, but the machine gun fire was too intense. As an assault crossing in boats was being planned a civilian ran across the bridge with the news that the Germans were withdrawing from the town. The carrier platoon commander, Lieutenant J. F. R. Burchell, was first across, closely followed by Major Miller with Prince of Wales Company, who killed or captured about 30 of the retreating Germans. Next across were Nos 3 and 4 Companies, who took up positions covering the main exits from the town.

Meanwhile the Sappers had arrived and were busy repairing the bridge. As this would take some time, Miller set about organizing a temporary bridge with the help of a crowd of townspeople, notably some local bargees who manoeuvred nine of their barges into position to form a makeshift pontoon bridge. But although Miller got his company jeep across, a burst of shellfire scattered the civilian helpers, and it was soon clear that the Germans were infiltrating back into Beeringen.

While the bridge was being repaired, No 2 Squadron (Major J. O. Spencer), patrolling southwards, met and fired on a large party of Germans, who turned out to be Hitler Youth. About 70 of them, some no more than 15 years old, crying for shame, gave themselves up—an odd, wretched incident.

In spite of increasing shellfire the Sappers worked on the bridge through the night, and by 4 a.m. it was strong enough to carry tanks. The leading group, No 1 Squadron and No 3 Company, were sniped at in the town and beyond it, and as they pushed on to Helchtern it became apparent that the wild chase to Brussels was not to be repeated. The Germans had recovered something of their balance, and were again capable of providing a coherent defence. But the Welsh Guards had been told to push on at any cost, with the result that by evening a running battle developed from Beeringen to Hechtel, the Welshmen striving to get forward, the

Germans counter-attacking wherever they could along the length of the road.

After leaving Beeringen the leading group were fired on by three self-propelled guns, but a tank dealt with one of them and No 3 Company dismounted and dealt with the other two. A little further on they ran into a German battalion forming up beside the road. Driving past, guns ablaze, they virtually destroyed it, killing or wounding several hundred and taking 150 prisoners. In Helchteren itself they were shot at, but pushed on another four miles to Hechtel, where No 1 Squadron was halted by anti-tank guns, losing one tank. No 3 Company tried to deal with them, but dusk was falling, and they ran into heavy fire from a number of machine gun posts.

Meanwhile behind them a second squadron/company group (No 3 Squadron and No 4 Company) had taken up positions covering Helchteren, awaiting the result of the fighting at Hechtel in front and Beeringen behind, where X Company, Scots Guards, were heavily engaged. Later in the afternoon they were relieved by the Irish Guards who had to deal with yet further counter-attacks as the Germans continued to reinforce the town. But it allowed X Company and the rest of the Welsh Group to concentrate forward at Helchteren. At about ten o'clock that night No 1 Squadron and No 3 Company, temporarily foiled at Hechtel, retired on the main body.

The following morning, 8 September, the battle proper for Hechtel started. The attack on Hechtel was first renewed by Prince of Wales and X Companies, supported by No 2 Squadron. But soon after they left the Germans started a series of counter-attacks on Helchteren. As on the previous day, the Welsh Guards Group was fighting in two places at once, several miles apart. Luckily the attacks were not co-ordinated, but launched piecemeal, and in each case were broken up with heavy casualties. Just before dark the Welsh were relieved by the Irish Guards, as they had been at

Beeringen, and again the Welsh Group was released for action further forward.

When Prince of Wales and X Companies had renewed the attack on Hechtel, they avoided the direct approach up the main road and came in from the west, astride the road from Bourg Leopold, with X Company on the left and Prince of Wales on the right. X Company made good progress through close country, driving in a number of outposts and destroying a self-propelled gun, to establish their leading platoons on the north and northeast outskirts of the town, with the third platoon in reserve.

Prince of Wales Company had more open country to contend with. They dealt with one machine gun post, but were then held up by a number of others. Miller therefore led them up the more covered approach already followed by X Company. They reached the edge of the village and moved back to the right flank, but were unable to get further than the main road. Throughout the day both companies had been closely supported by No 2 Squadron, under Major Spencer; and it was while Miller and Spencer were reconnoitring their next move, that the Germans put in a counter-attack. It was driven off, but by now it was getting dark, and Miller decided to consolidate for the night on the right of X Company's reserve platoon.

During the night the enemy made repeated efforts to infiltrate both companies' positions. For the most part these attempts were defeated, but they did succeed in establishing themselves between X Company's forward and rear platoons. An enemy patrol also managed to penetrate No 2 Squadron's headquarters and killed Major Spencer. Spencer was an older man who could have had a perfectly honourable war in a less arduous position than that of a tank squadron commander. But he chose not to do so, and he proved himself a fine and well loved leader who would be sadly missed.

The following day, the 9th, No 3 Company attacked on the right of Prince of Wales, but failed to get further than the

Western limits of the town. A number of casualties were incurred, including Major H. E. J. Lister, commanding Support Company, who was killed. Like Spencer, Lister was a man who could have chosen an easier war. He was an ordained priest of the Church of England, but he preferred as a matter of faith to take an active part in what he considered a fight against evil.

Later in the day a strong counter-attack by the enemy succeeded in dislodging some of the forward sections of both Prince of Wales and No 3 Companies. Although the situation was soon restored, it showed how vulnerable was the position of X Company's forward platoons. They had already been isolated for 24 hours and the Company Commander now ordered them to withdraw on to his reserve platoon. Their record in the Beeringen–Hechtel fight had been a particularly splendid one. They were in close contact with the enemy for four days, repelled two counter-attacks and had been twice surrounded. But inspired by the leadership of Major Steuart-Fotheringham, they gave no ground until at last he ordered them to do so.

The following day the three companies in Hechtel, Prince of Wales, X Company and No 3 tried to work their way forward. But Hechtel had been reinforced, and that night the Germans again managed to get in between the forward positions in the town. Lance-Corporal T. Kennedy, in charge of ten prisoners in one house, had at one stage Germans in the houses on either side. Nevertheless he kept the prisoners quiet and the Germans out, and on the following day, when the houses were once more regained, he emerged with his prisoners intact. Later that day the 11th, No 4 Company, attacked along the main road from the south; although they linked up with No 3 Company, they could get no further.

Hechtel was proving a tough nut to crack, and the Coldstream at Bourg Leopold were also held up. But Guards Armoured Division had been ordered to get on and take a bridge over the Escaut Canal at any price. Accordingly, on the 9th, the Household Cavalry slipped through between Hechtel and Bourg Leopold, scarcely a mile to the west of Hechtel, followed by the regimental groups of the Grenadier and Irish Guards. By the evening of the 10th they had secured the desired crossing at the de Groot Barrier bridge, having taken the Germans completely by surprise.

But Hechtel still held out, although with the *coup* by the Grenadier and Irish Guards at de Groot it was virtually surrounded. It was decided that on the 12th a full scale, co-ordinated attack by both the Welsh Guards battalions would be mounted, supported by the mortars, machine guns and anti-tank guns of the 1st Battalion, the machine guns and mortars of the Northumberland Fusiliers,[1] and the medium guns of the 11th Armoured Division. The Guards' Divisional artillery had already gone forward in support of the bridge-head at de Groot. In order to allow full freedom to the barrage, the companies were withdrawn during the night, which also allowed them to reform for the attack which was to take place on two axes, from the south and from the west.

The barrage came down at 8 a.m., and at 8.30 Nos 3 and 4 Companies, supported by Nos 1 and 3 Squadrons, attacked along the main road. Progress was a slow house-to-house business, but inexorable with the tanks shooting up each point of resistance. By midday they had reached the cross-roads at the centre of the town. At that moment Prince of Wales and X Companies came in at right-angles along the Bourg Leopold road, and by 1 p.m. Hechtel had fallen.

This final attack was a sweeping success: 150 German dead were counted, 220 wounded were evacuated, and 500 prisoners were taken, including their skilful and defiant commander, Captain Muller. Unfortunately Muller's soldierly qualities did not redeem his brutal behaviour in other

---

[1] This Company, armed with heavy machine guns and mortars, gave invaluable help to the Guards Armoured Division throughout the campaign. The Northumberland Fusiliers provided similar companies for both the 7th and 11th Armoured Divisions.

respects. He had had shot eleven civilians, seemingly for no better reason than that they had annoyed him. Those who survived a burst of machine gun fire were finished off with grenades in a cellar, where their remains were subsequently found. In due course Muller was tried and convicted as a war criminal by the Belgian Government.

By capturing the bridge over the Escaut Canal and prising open the routes up to it at Hechtel and Bourg Leopold, an operation described by the Corps Commander as 'brilliant— a word I don't often use', the Guards Armoured Division opened the way for the plan now maturing in Field-Marshal Montgomery's mind. He had already intended to advance to, and if possible over, the Rhine, west of the Ruhr. He now proposed a bolder stroke, to cut right through from Eindhoven to the Zuider Zee, outflanking the Siegfried Line and getting into the industrial Ruhr by the back door. Had he succeeded the war might have been over in 1944.

1st and 2nd Battalions:
Holland—Operation Market Garden

From the Escaut to the Rhine at Arnhem is 50 miles. To get there would involve crossing three major and five lesser rivers or canals. British and American Airborne Forces were to capture, intact, as many bridges as possible over these waterways. This part of the operation, code-named Market, was commanded by a Grenadier, General Browning. The other half of the operation, code-named Garden, was for XXX Corps to relieve, in succession, each precariously held crossing. The spearhead of XXX Corps was Guards Armoured Division.

Orders were given out on 16 September, and confirmed at midnight. The drop started at 1330 on the 17th, the Division moving off half an hour later. At first all went well. Indeed the performance of the Household Cavalry far out ahead, and then of the Irish, and later the Grenadier Battle Groups, was little short of inspired. The Irish rumbled along at a steady 8 mph, behind a tremendous barrage that rolled forward at the same speed. That evening, after a brief fight, the bridge at Walkensward was captured intact. The following day they reached Eindhoven, which was firmly in the hands of 101 US Airborne Division. The bridge there too was intact, so they pushed on to Zon. There the bridge was blown, but it was repaired overnight, and next day the advance continued with the Grenadiers in the lead. By 0830 they had crossed the Maas at Grave, where 82nd US Airborne had captured another unblown bridge. That evening they were in the outskirts of Nijmegen.

Here the Americans were not yet in full control, and it was not until the following evening that the Grenadiers, fighting hard with 505 US Parachute Battalion under command, cleared their way to the bridge. Then in the failing light came the tense moment when four Grenadier tanks revved up their engines and dashed across the bridge, which at any moment could have been blown under them. It seemed a long time before they signalled their arrival on the other side. Two companies of Irish Guards then followed them across and were able to establish a restricted bridgehead. Sporadic and bitter fighting continued for the rest of the night. The German defence was fanatical to the last, leaving 400 of their dead on or around the bridge.

The Welsh Group meanwhile had been guarding the Grave area, which was still vulnerable to counter-attack. The wisdom of this precaution became very apparent later when the centre-line was twice cut by the Germans, delaying vital supplies and equipment, assault boats particularly, which added another adverse factor to the relief of Arnhem.

On the 21st the Welsh Guards were called forward to help in the advance from Nijmegen to Arnhem, now tantalizingly close, its spires, less than ten miles away, visible across the flat, marshy ground. But it was at this last stretch between the rivers Waal and Rhine, which came to be known as 'The Island', that the difficulties of this curious fen-like country became decisive. 'The Island' was barely reclaimed marshland. The main road is raised well above the surrounding polder, itself criss-crossed with dykes, so that the tanks were at once perfect targets on the road, and at the same time unable to get off it.

The Irish led from the bridgehead along the main road, but were soon held up by an anti-tank screen at Elst. The Welsh Guards prodded down a subsidiary road to the west in an outflanking movement towards Oosterhout. But although the leading troop, under Lieutenant M. C. Devas, knocked out three German tanks, and although the Irish were in striking distance of Bemel, the centre of German resistance, it was now getting dark. The Corps Commander decided that the attack on Arnhem was an infantry and not an armoured task, and that before it could succeed the bridgehead must be expanded. That night both Irish and Welsh Guards were withdrawn to pivotal positions around the bridgehead. The following day the attack was continued by the 43rd Infantry Division.

On the 23rd the 1st Battalion, supported by a squadron of the 2nd Battalion, started to enlarge the bridgehead by attacking towards Bemel: Prince of Wales Company and X Companies were in the lead, with No 3 Company in reserve. No 4 Company had been temporarily disbanded after the losses at Hechtel. Both forward companies captured their objectives, with about ten casualties each.

This was a depressing time. It had started to rain heavily, and continued to do so for a large part of the time that the battalions spent on 'The Island'. But worse still, the great objective of Arnhem, so near and yet so far, had still not been relieved and the situation of its defenders was known to be desperate. Including the Guards Armoured Division there were now three divisions on 'The Island', but for all their efforts the glittering prize remained just out of reach, and on the night of 25/26 September the gallant remnant of the British Airborne Forces had to be withdrawn across the Rhine.

On the 26th the Welsh Group were ordered to take over the village of Aam and from there push a company forward. So No 3 Company, under Major W. D. D. Evans, advanced for nearly two miles supported by two troops of tanks from No 1 Squadron. They reached the main dyke which runs in front of Aam and faces Arnhem itself, and that night they patrolled along the dyke without incident. The following day they were involved in one of those useless and wasteful operations sometimes thrown up in war. About half a mile along the dyke, the map showed a considerable bridge; the Company's position would obviously be stronger if the bridge was in its hands. They were, accordingly, told to attack this site, which they did at a cost of several casualties, both killed and wounded. But when they got there, they found that the bridge no longer existed. The Company was told to withdraw, and a small but difficult action with strong artillery and mortar support was required before they could extricate themselves.

That night the battalions were relieved by the Irish Guards, and until 6 October were constantly on call against German counter-attacks, which remained frequent and vicious. Squadrons of the 2nd Battalion in particular were 'hired out daily', as the Commanding Officer put it, in support of infantry battalions fighting off these attacks. But neither battalion was heavily involved, and casualties on 'The Island' were mercifully light. However it must have been an unusual, as well as a sad and proud, moment when Sergeant A. E. Hervey, of the 2nd Battalion, attended the burial of his son, Guardsman J. A. Hervey, who was killed serving with the 1st Battalion. On 6 October the Guards Armoured Division was withdrawn for a well-deserved rest, and the battalions went to Malden, four miles south of Nijmegen.

With hindsight there are many might-have-beens about the Arnhem campaign. It almost succeeded, was well worth the attempt and the failure was narrow. But as with all really bold adventures when the stakes are high, success had to be complete; in this case it was not, and there are no consolation prizes in war. Only the record of the troops on the ground can be quoted without reservation or afterthought. The stand of the Airborne Division at Arnhem was epic; and the advance of the Guards Armoured Division from the Escaut Canal to relieve them, was as memorable a feat of arms as any in the long history of the Household Division.

1st and 2nd Battalions:
Winter in Belgium and Holland

After their withdrawal from 'The Island', the battalions remained in the Malden area for nearly a month. They had been in almost continuous action since they had started on the triumphal advance on Brussels, and were badly in need of rest, reinforcement and refitment.

Lieutenant-Colonel C. H. R. Heber-Percy, now recovered from his wound in Normandy, resumed command of the 1st Battalion while it was still on 'The Island' and during their stay at Malden the Battalion received sufficient reinforcements to be able to reform No 4 Company. X Company still remained with them, but the Company Commander, Major Steuart-Fotheringham, was posted elsewhere. On 12 October representatives of both battalions were present at a Divisional Parade for the King who was visiting his troops in the area.

All units of the Division, now in counter-attack reserve, were allotted roles in case of need, but for the most part they were not called upon to fulfil them. These duties were light enough to allow leave to Brussels where a Welsh Guardsman lacked for nothing. Excellent football fields were available, and matches were played against some good Dutch teams, as well as against other battalions. The Division also returned, with some relief, to British rations. During the struggle on 'The Island', lines of communication had twice been cut; rations and NAAFI stores had been hard to come by, the shortfall being made good from a captured German supply depot. The German soldier's standard of living was patently inferior to that of the British, and acorn coffee no substitute for char.

On 4 November the 1st Battalion moved south to relieve an infantry battalion at Veulen. Contact with the enemy was close and they had to take over the battered little village in the dark. The weather was beastly; it rained almost without ceasing and rain and mud are the principal memories of this sector of the line. There was also a good deal of shelling and mortaring by the Germans.

Nevertheless an aggressive programme of patrolling was carried out. On one occasion Lieutenant D. J. C. Stevenson, after establishing a standing patrol in a farm building, continued to reconnoitre forward and shot a German officer who declined to surrender. He then killed another who came to see what was going on. Stevenson, and Guardsman Evans who was with him, then returned to the farm to find it almost surrounded by the enemy. Stevenson extricated the patrol with some difficulty, and on his way back surprised and scattered a further party of Germans who were laying mines.

The next day, 7 November, a daylight raid was carried out by a party of 15 from Prince of Wales Company, under the command of Lieutenant D. Bruce. The plan was to attack a house known to be occupied by the enemy, and having driven them out to booby-trap it; for this purpose a section of the pioneer platoon was attached to the raiding party. Lance-Sergeant L. A. R. Webb, commanding the leading section, reached the house under heavy fire. Bruce had almost joined him when he was severely wounded. Webb crawled back to

Bruce and applied a field dressing, but two stretcher-bearers who tried to rescue him were also wounded. Webb managed to drag Bruce to temporary safety. That achieved he continued the attack on the house, drove out the enemy and planted the booby-traps as planned. Finally he withdrew the patrol, still under heavy fire, taking with him Bruce and six other wounded.

On 12 November the Division moved to the Maastricht area, where they were to remain for the next five weeks, the longest period they were to spend in any one place during the campaign. The Welsh Guards Group were posted forward of Sittard, in the two villages of Millen and Tuddern. Sittard, a neat little Dutch town, was only 4,000 yards away from the front line, but life there went on normally. The two villages were just over the border, and for the first time the Welsh Guards found themselves on German soil. There was some patrolling and shelling, but this was a quiet part of the front.

The only noteworthy attempt by the Germans to make themselves felt came one evening when Guardsmen Lloyd and Brookes, quietly frying chips in their billet, were surprised by an enemy patrol which tried to march them off. The Guardsmen were unarmed, but fists and feet prevailed. Although the Germans fired at them, wounding Brookes, both Brookes and Lloyd escaped.

On 16 December orders were given for the Division to withdraw from the battle zone to a rest area near Louvain. After staging on the way both Welsh Guards battalions reached their billets on the 21st, the 1st Battalion at Hougaerde and the 2nd at Jodoigne. They were only 25 miles from Brussels and had orders to make themselves comfortable for Christmas. But on the 16th the Germans had launched their last desperate fling against the Allies. The weight of their attack, by 14 infantry and 10 panzer divisions, was concentrated on the Americans in the Ardennes, and in much of the hard fighting the Division's old friends, the

American 82nd and 101st Airborne Divisions, again distinguished themselves.

The Guards Division's rest area suddenly became a concentration area, conveniently placed to cover the approaches to Brussels should that become necessary. It did not, but as a precautionary measure the Welsh Group was moved to Namur and the neighbouring high ground overlooking the Meuse. It was appropriate that among the first to arrive should be X Company, Scots Guards—Namur had been their Regiment's first Battle Honour in 1695. But by the end of the year the Americans had the attack under control and the tide turned. The Germans had proved that they were still a dangerous enemy, but their gamble had achieved little except the loss of irreplaceable men and equipment.

On 29 December both battalions returned to their delayed Christmas dinners at Hougaerde and Jodoigne. There they were to remain until February, making friends with their hospitable Belgian hosts. Towards the end of January rumours of the next great battle began to filter down to the battalions. At the end of that month also the Division was joined by the 2nd Battalion, Scots Guards, who were eventually to relieve the 1st Battalion, Welsh Guards, who were not expected to be able to sustain the necessary reinforcement rate to replace the casualties foreseen in the next bout of hard fighting. Meanwhile the 2nd Scots Guards would be able to gain experience of fighting with an armoured division before teaming up with the 2nd Battalion, Welsh Guards, in a new Scots–Welsh Group.

3rd Battalion: Winter in Italy

The winter campaign of the 3rd Battalion began on 2 October and lasted until the middle of February 1945, and was conducted 2,000 feet up, in the mud, snow and cold of the Apennine mountains. The map gives little idea of the wild confusion of the steep ridges and spurs, valleys and re-entrants of this bad-tempered geological formation.

The Battalion's first entry into these bleak mountains was not too bad, though the long haul up to their first position on Monte Battaglia took seven hours. At least the ground was dry; thereafter it rained relentlessly, a chill rain that turned to snow as the winter progressed.

Battaglia itself is the high point of a long, twisting ridge, and on the summit lay the ruins of an old castle which, like the castle at Cassino, could only be reached with the aid of ropes stapled into the mountainside. The final approach was along a knife-edge with an abrupt fall on either side. In some places the ridge was so narrow that it could only be negotiated with one's feet on either side of it, a balancing act made more difficult by high winds, driving rain and enemy mortar fire. The German positions were perched behind the castle, where the ridge continued and branched into a number of subsidiary ridges.

This was mountain warfare with a vengeance, with all the attendant difficulties of getting supplies up and wounded down. However casualties were mercifully fewer than they had been on Cerasola the year before, but it was still a three to four hour carry by relays of stretcher bearers back to the road, down the single, steep, muddy and sometimes icy track. The journey up was equally arduous, and the 150 mules and 100 men who made the trek up and down each night with supplies, did nothing to improve the going. Also, as the British advanced their positions, gradually pushing the Germans back, so the nightly trek became longer.

When 1st Guards Brigade relieved the American troops, the 3rd Battalion took over the defences of the causeway, the Coldstream took over the southeast slopes, and the Grenadiers the castle and the area round it. The many bodies, American and German, were stark evidence of how bitterly the Germans had contested the advance of the Americans on to Battaglia.

The Battalion's positions lay back in considerable depth along the causeway, and although there were standing patrols to cover the inevitable gaps, there was always the danger of the enemy sneaking up one of the hidden gulleys between them. But the layout of the companies proved to be good. At first light on the 11th they were attacked by the 1st Battalion of 577 GR Regiment. An Operation Order and a marked map, picked up after the attack, showed that the enemy objectives were exactly those features the Battalion held. The first sign of trouble came when Captain A. J. S. Cassavetti of No 4 Company was returning from a visit to the castle, which he was due to take over from the Grenadiers the following night. After being challenged by Lieutenant W. A. O. J. Bell's platoon on point 647, Cassavetti, and the small party with him, ran into a number of Germans. Cassavetti's party got safely in, Bell's platoon killing four of the enemy.

At five in the morning the first attack fell on Canovaccia, where some of the Germans tried to force their way into the farmyard. But they were driven off by a section of No 3 Company, under Lance-Corporal D. F. Burgess, at point-blank range, which tumbled them back down the hillside to La Briole. There another wave of attackers was met by Lieutenant J. T. Jerman's platoon, who had held their fire, expecting one of their own standing patrols to pass back through them. When they did open up the results were all the more devastating, and the Germans were driven off. The Germans also got close to a Grenadier mortar position 200 yards away. But Jerman and the Grenadiers between them dealt with that matter too.

British 3-inch mortars put down defensive fire in front of No 3 Company and No 1 Company could also fire effectively across their front. In return, a little later, No 3 Company were able to warn No 1 of an impending attack on their position. Again the Germans pressed their attack close to No 1 Company's slit-trenches; again they were driven off by heavy machine gun and rifle fire and were forced to take cover in a house further down the valley. The house immediately came under mortar and machine gun fire from both Welsh and Grenadier Guards, and quite soon a German appeared with a Red Cross flag. He approached No 1 Company and asked for an armistice to remove the wounded. He was given half an hour, but warned that if his force did not surrender, the house and all in it would be destroyed. In the event the Germans were given a little longer and after 45 minutes an officer and 74 men came out with their hands up. It was learned from these prisoners that the attack which had ended in confusion had also started badly. Their companies had got lost in the dark and then got themselves hopelessly mixed up in the jagged country.

That night, as planned, the Battalion took over responsibility for the castle area from the Grenadiers. The castle itself was held by 16 men in the keep; the old, thick walls made it safe enough, but it was a thoroughly unpleasant position. There could be no movement by day, the garrison having to exist cheek by jowl with the remains of those who fought there before them. But the Germans made no further attempts to take the castle, and when the Battalion returned there on 19 October after a short spell in billets, the enemy had withdrawn. As the Germans were followed up, the castle became, in due course, a rear position.

On 25 October the Battalion left the Battaglia sector and crossed the Santerno valley to the mountains on the other side, where conditions were much the same. The weather remained vile. They remained in the Verro area until 31 October and little of note occurred. But when newspapers and even official despatches say they have nothing to report, there is always a battle for someone. On the 28th Lance-Sergeant E. Hart, who was commanding a platoon of No 4 Company, was told by an Italian peasant that the Germans were using a house in the hamlet of La Costa, a few hundred yards away. As Hart was asking instructions from his

Company Commander over the field telephone, the cable was cut by shellfire. At the same moment a mist came down. Hart saw his opportunity, and without waiting for further orders rushed the house with a small party and came back with four prisoners. The next day Lance-Sergeant J. McGhan was sent out with a fighting patrol of six men with orders to occupy the house and hold it during the night. On the way out he scattered a German patrol before establishing himself in the house. At about three in the morning a strong enemy patrol tried to rush the house. They managed to get a grenade through a window, wounding McGhan and three of his men. But they fought off the raid, and at first light McGhan, in spite of his own painfully wounded leg, got his patrol, including the wounded, safely back to base.

At the end of the month the Battalion was relieved and moved into a succession of billets in the Salerno and Senio valleys. On the 11th they moved back to Battaglia for the last time. On the 18th they moved to billets in Greve, only 15 miles from Florence.

During the next three months a routine was developed by which companies spent alternate periods of four or five days in Greve or in the mountains. From Greve it was an easy step to Florence and in both places they made friends, in Florence giving a ball to repay the kindness of their many hostesses. If the arrangement was something less than the complete retirement to winter quarters which the sensible convention of bygone armies allowed, it was a reasonable compromise which made bearable the well-nigh intolerable conditions in the mountains. Even there things improved a little; winter clothing of windsuits, string vests, Alpine pullovers and thick white socks was issued, all of which helped to reduce the incidence of frostbite and trench feet compared with the previous year. But nobody ever did discover how to keep melting snow out of a boot.

From December until February the Battalion held positions along the Penzola ridge, on Monte dell'Acqua Salata, and finally on Monte del Verro. Each position was a little further north than the previous one, so lengthening the nightly journey of the mule train. But in spite of the difficulties of ice, mud and reluctant Indian muleteers, Captain J. J. Gurney and the Guardsmen responsible for supply never left the companies seriously short of their requirements. It was a Herculean achievement.

On 14 February the Battalion slogged up to Verro for the last time. The next night there was considerable shelling and mortar fire, especially on the forward positions of No 4 Company (Major J. D. Gibson-Watt). Later two platoons, under Lieutenant D. G. Cottom, were attacked by about 20 German paratroopers. However the reception proved too hot for them, and after 20 minutes they broke off the action, leaving a number of dead behind.

At last, on 17 February, the 3rd Battalion, Welsh Guards, left the mountains for the last time after an exhausting winter. No great battles had been fought, no action had made the headlines. But success in this tough, dour and all too often unrecorded soldiering is as great a test of morale, skill and leadership, especially by junior officers and NCOs, as any ringing victory.

6 THE SECOND WORLD WAR: 1945

1st and 2nd Battalions: the Reichswald Forest

The overall intention of the forthcoming battle was to clear the enemy completely from the country between the Maas and the Rhine. First Canadian Army, backed by XXX Corps with Guards Armoured Division in reserve, was to strike southeast from the line Mook–Nijmegen. The objective of the Division was Wesel. Because of the speed of their Cromwell tanks, once the Reichswald Forest had been cleared, the Welsh Group was to lead, and if possible grab the Wesel bridge over the Rhine intact—if by some heaven-sent chance it had not been blown. The other aim of the operation, code-named Veritable, was to draw off the German reserves facing the American First and Ninth Armies, who were to advance northwards from Aachen to meet the British. Because of the number of enemy agents known to be at large, the operation was planned and mounted in the greatest secrecy, though an inkling that something was afoot was gained when the field gunners set off in advance with their unit signs carefully painted off their vehicles.

The first attacks, which started on 8 February, went as planned, supported by the heaviest artillery barrage of the war. Over 1,000 guns fired half a million shells in five and a half hours on a seven-mile front. But the weather, bad from the start, broke completely after a couple of days. The frozen ground thawed, roads were flooded, and an all pervasive and reluctant mud allowed little movement by either tracked or wheeled vehicles. On one occasion the only way to move part of the Division was by a bone-shaking drive along the sleepers of a railway track. Furthermore the start of the American attack had to be postponed for a fortnight because the Germans had opened the Roer dams and flooded the American area of operations.

Veritable had now become a slow, slogging infantry battle, and the original plan for a quick advance had to be abandoned. It was now 13 February and 32nd Guards Brigade was sent for, not in the by now accustomed form of Regimental Groups, but as an infantry brigade of three battalions, with tank support from 2nd Battalion, Welsh Guards. The Reichswald Forest had been cleared, but there were no troops over the River Nieder, except for 51st Highland Division at Gennap; 32nd Guards Brigade were put under its command to extend the bridgehead to the village of Hommersum.

The Brigade plan for the 14th was for the 5th Battalion, Coldstream Guards, and 1st Battalion, Welsh Guards, to take the woods northwest of Hommersum, and for the Irish Guards, supported by No 2 Squadron, Welsh Guards, to pass through and take the village itself. The operation started at 3.30 in the afternoon, and was completed punctually. Seventy-eight prisoners were taken, the few casualties mostly being suffered by the Welsh Guards who ran into a lot of mines in the wood.

Although the attack had gone like clockwork, the Germans objected almost at once with a strong fighting patrol that night. This was followed by a small but determined counter-attack the next day, heavily supported by artillery. But British casualties were few and the attack was driven off. No 2 Squadron was also engaged again that day further north, in support of an attack by the Black Watch on Kessel.

On the 16th No 1 Squadron, Welsh Guards, under Major
N. T. L. Fisher, supported the Coldstream in a successful
attack on Mull. But for the tanks it was a frustrating day.
The ground, which had looked firm enough, turned out to be
a morass under a deceitful crust. Of the 19 tanks which went
into action, 17 were bogged down. Major Fisher, himself
unhorsed by the foundering mud in one tank, mounted
another which blew up on a mine. Then although wounded
he led his two remaining tanks on to the objective on foot.

That night the 1st Battalion attacked Hassum, a large
village on the road to Goch. They had the advantage of
artificial moonlight; also the attack was preceded by an air
attack of some weight and a considerable barrage by the
artillery. They started from the positions they had taken on
the 14th and lost two killed and four wounded as they left
the shelter of the wood. They then dug in forward of
Hommersum, now held by the Irish Guards, and at three in
the morning went into the final assault. It was a walkover.
They reached the ruins of Hassum without further casualties
and easily flushed out the remnants of the garrison: nine
rather miserable specimens of the 'Master Race'. But as they
consolidated there was some heavy shellfire, and Lieutenant
R. J. S. Howard of X Company was wounded. As soon as it
was daylight patrols were pushed out to gain contact with
the enemy. Lieutenant E. M. Ling brought news that the
bridge at Terporten was intact. Other patrols brought in
useful information—one under Lieutenant J. S. Roberts from
No 3 Company brought in seven dozen eggs as well.

The 1st Battalion remained in the Hassum area for a
fortnight, engaged in a busy programme of patrolling and
some minor operations, in which they were supported by the
Light Reconnaissance Squadron of the 2nd Battalion, which
was not otherwise engaged during this period. Indeed the
Welsh Group had a run of luck in that they were not committed to any of the intense fighting that involved other units
of the Division at this time. Casualties were light, although

when Major W. D. D. Evans was wounded he was sadly missed by the Battalion as well as by No 4 Company, which he had commanded with such distinction since Normandy.

On 2 March 32nd Guards Brigade rejoined the Division; the Regimental Group system was re-established and the 1st and 2nd Battalions married up at Siebengewald. The objective of the Guards Armoured Division was to exploit the advance of XXX Corps eastward from Kevellear towards Wesel, where the Germans were making a last-ditch stand west of the Rhine and forward of a road running parallel to it. A successful attack by 5th Guards Brigade to Kevellear and beyond, put the wooded high ground of Bonninghardt within striking distance. From there a forward slope ran down to the road and the river.

On 5 March the Welsh Group, together with the 2nd Battalion Scots Guards, had orders to attack first the Bonninghardt woods and then, if all went well, to go on and take the village itself. At eleven o'clock on the 6th the start-line was crossed. The 1st Battalion, Welsh Guards, were responsible for the right half of the wood and the 2nd Battalion, Scots Guards, for the left. Both were supported by a squadron of the 2nd Battalion, Welsh Guards. They also had strong artillery support, and by keeping up to the barrage they were able to fight their way through the woods, where denser growth made close tank support difficult. There were tough pockets of resistance from German paratroopers, but by midday the wood was clear. They had taken nearly 100 prisoners, at a cost of 37 wounded.

Soon after they reached their objective Lieutenant-Colonel Heber-Percy ordered the second part of the advance, on to Bonninghardt village. No 3 Company led on the right, supported by No 3 Squadron, and on the left X Company were supported by the Light Reconnaissance Squadron. They again had strong artillery support. There were casualties to start with crossing open ground, but after some hand-to-hand fighting the village was taken. During the night it was

completely cleared and 50 more Germans were winkled out
and taken prisoner. One of them almost had the last word in
an exchange with Regimental Sergeant-Major Baker. In
answer to the somewhat traditional query, 'And what do you
think you're laughing at?' he replied, 'Well, I've finished
with the war, which is more than you have.' But he was not
quite right, after all. Except for a flank-guard attack a couple
of days later by No 4 Company, in support of the 2nd Scots
Guards, when they reached their objective without loss, the
1st Battalion, Welsh Guards, had fought their last battle of
the war.

But for the 2nd Battalion there was still work to do. About
two miles beyond the Bonninghardt feature lay the road
which followed the west bank of the Rhine. If that were cut it
would so disrupt the German communications that their
resistance in the Wesel bridgehead would collapse. A mile
short of the road two embanked railway lines crossed each
other at right-angles. As a first step to cutting the road, the
2nd Battalion, Scots Guards, with No 2 Squadron, Welsh
Guards, in support, were ordered to capture the apex
formed by the two railway lines.

The attack started at 4.30 on the afternoon of 7 March.
The first obstacle was a stream at the foot of the slope down
from Bonninghardt. Over the stream was a small farm
bridge, strong enough for tanks, but just too narrow. Major
Daniel coaxed some of his Cromwells across, but the tracks
ground away the edges of the bridge and weakened it.
However at that moment a scissors bridge (mounted on a
tank) appeared, and the Squadron got over the stream without further delay. Meanwhile the Scots Guards companies
had pushed on to the railway lines, but darkness fell before
the tanks could help them establish themselves effectively for
the night. It was an uncomfortable position. The infantry dug
themselves in as well as they could, and Daniel with No 2
Squadron had to harbour forward. A hundred and six
prisoners had been taken, but resistance continued throughout

the night. Shelling and mortar fire was heavy, accurate and unceasing. Two tanks were lost by shellfire and Lieutenant P. A. Carter and Lance-Sergeant H. J. Millard were killed. At first light four more tanks were knocked out by a self-propelled gun which had got in behind the squadron. Meanwhile Mechanist Quartermaster-Sergeant F. Roughton had laboured all night under fire to free a tank on the scissors bridge, and the Sappers had thrown a Bailey bridge over the stream nearby. Both were needed for the final effort against Wesel. That day, after one of their heaviest battles of the war, the Coldstream Group cut the vital road, and by evening all German resistance west of the Rhine came to an end.

On 11 March the Division was withdrawn for rest, again to the Nijmegen area. And there the 1st Battalion left the division which they had been among the first to join. On 18 March they held a farewell parade in the Nijmegen stadium, and then for the last time marched past their general. Five days later they entrained for England at Nijmegen station, where a large crowd of their comrades of the Guards Armoured Division had assembled to wave them farewell.

3rd Battalion: the Po and the Adige

After they left the cold winter mountains the 3rd Battalion had two months in which to prepare for the final thrust in Italy. They returned to Greve for five days, then they went to Spoleto, and finally they spent three weeks at Porto San Georgio, where they bathed, fished and sailed in the clear waters of the Adriatic, under the warm sunshine of the Italian spring. On 7 April they were visited there by the Regimental Lieutenant-Colonel, Sir Alexander Stanier, who had recently commanded 231st Infantry Brigade in Normandy and Belgium. While there he spoke to each company, and saw all officers and NCOs down to the rank of sergeant, individually.

On 9 April the Battalion had orders to move at four o'clock the next morning. They were seen firmly on their way by Lieutenant-Colonel J. E. Gurney, who had commanded them for ten months, and who now had to leave for a staff job on the 12th. The Battalion was commanded by Major J. R. Martin-Smith until the 22nd, when Lieutenant-Colonel R. C. Rose Price took over at the decisive moment of the battle.

The opening moves of Field-Marshal Alexander's great sweep, which was to destroy the German armies in Italy, had already started. As a preliminary the 8th Army had gained a bridgehead over the Senio River on 2 April. The main battle started on the 8th. On the right the 8th Army made a punch across the Santerno to seize the Argenta gap, the only solid going between the confluence of the five rivers Reno, Idice, Sillaro, Santerno and Senio, and the lagoon of Lake Comachio. They were to make for the Po at Ferrara and Bondeno. Further to the west, the 5th Army was to descend from the mountains, capture Bologna and make for the Po via Finale. The aim of both armies was to reach the Po before the Germans could establish a line of defence there, and this was achieved.

Initially the 6th Armoured Division was in 8th Army reserve, and for the first ten days they moved up behind the advancing line of battle, waiting for their chance. It came on 20 April. The Argenta gap had been secured, and 26th Armoured Brigade, with the 3rd Battalion, was ordered to break out. The first results were disappointing; resistance was met after only 400 yards, from positions which had been reported as being in Allied hands. No 1 Company was the first to be committed, and then the others in turn. But by evening the Battalion had positions on the north bank of the Reno from Traghetto to Borgo Cortili. There was some fighting, but casualties were light; they took about 40 prisoners and 100 more the next day. From that day on the hunt was up and there was no stopping the 6th Armoured Division. However there was still some stout resistance, particularly at the next water obstacle, the Combalina Canal. The 1st Battalion, the Welch Regiment (who had replaced the Coldstream in 1st Guards Brigade), made an assault crossing, but were counter-attacked by armour before they had consolidated. But the 17th/21st Lancers found an unblown bridge further along the canal, rushed it, and pushed on for five miles until they were in rear of the Germans attacking the Welch Regiment. The Welch then made a second assault and crossed in strength, allowing the Grenadiers to pass forward.

The next day, the 22nd, the Armoured Brigade continued their advance, biting ever more deeply into the enemy's flank, cutting his lines of communication and destroying his columns, now retreating helter-skelter to the River Po. That evening they reached Mirabello, about ten miles beyond the Combalina Canal, where the 3rd Battalion was called for to clear the town. This was completed the following morning by No 1 Company (Major P. V. Makins), while the armour pushed on to Bondeno and Finale. A reconnaissance party from the Welsh Guards went ahead with them to ensure swift co-operation from the Battalion when needed.

A quick armoured advance produces a heady excitement and a flavour all its own: the billowing clouds of dust, the dejected columns of prisoners, burning vehicles, overturned guns and dead horses, charred and ruined houses. And in the middle of the destruction, frantically excited crowds pelting their liberators with flowers, and sometimes in their enthusiasm providing the only delay to the speeding troops. These were the scenes that met the Allied armies for the next few days as they rampaged through northern Italy, one after another of the ancient cities of the plain falling into their hands.

On the 23rd the leading tanks of 26th Armoured Brigade

met two jeeps driving towards them with cherry-coloured sheets on their bonnets; the 8th and the 5th Armies had met and the Germans south of the Po were encircled. The next day the Grenadiers made a quick crossing of the Po against light opposition, and early the following morning the Welsh Guards followed them over and pushed on. No 4 Company, under Major J. D. Gibson-Watt, made rapid progress. The country was flat and without hedges, though an occasional line of poplars stood like exclamation marks against the sky. But the country was scoured by a series of wide and defensible irrigation ditches which could not be taken for granted. Sergeant M. G. G. Chatwin, in command of the leading platoon, with great skill and courage made six quick attacks in five miles, and with the other platoons following made a deep bridgehead which was widened by the rest of the Battalion. Lieutenant-Colonel R. C. Rose Price was determined to exploit this success by driving straight on to capture the next bridge, which crossed the Bianca Canal at Castel Gugliemo, five miles ahead.

Sergeant Emrys Davies and his platoon, mounted on amphibious tanks, volunteered for the task. And led by the Commanding Officer himself, his gunner Major Grieg of the Ayrshire Yeomanry and Major Gibson-Watt in jeeps, the party made a dash for Castel Gugliemo. They got there just before dark and found the bridge intact. The Guardsmen, who had dismounted, opened fire on a German on the other side of the canal and a Very light went up on the gathering dusk. The leading tanks had just revved up preparatory to the dash across when, with a tremendous explosion, the bridge was blown in the troop commander's face. The spectacular dash had just failed. It was now dark, and since the Sappers were already bridging the canal at another point along the bank, there was nothing to be gained by continuing the foray and the party was ordered to pull back to the Battalion for the night.

The following day the advance continued towards the

Adige, with the Battalion following other units of the Division. The Welch Regiment by-passed Lendinara, which the Welsh Guards were ordered to clear. This was done after a brisk fight by the Carrier Platoon under Lieutenant J. J. Hoffman. A number of the enemy were killed or wounded and about 70 were taken prisoner.

The Battalion was then ordered on to the Adige. There, benefiting from the lessons learnt at Castel Gugliemo, the order was given that fire should not be directed across the river before any assault was made. But a German sniper, roosting on a twisted girder of the half-blown bridge, narrowly missed the Commanding Officer. And since another bridge had been found a few miles away, making it unnecessary for the Welsh Guards to force a crossing, the order was cancelled. The Battalion's own snipers then lined the bank and in due course opened fire on a party of 14 Germans, who for some reason tried to pick their way across the bridge towards them. One German was knocked off the bridge and three others were wounded. After a very brief conference they gave themselves up.

They did not know it at the time, but those shots, fired on the afternoon of 27 April, were the last to be fired by the 3rd Battalion, Welsh Guards, in the Second World War. To be sure there was now little left to fire at; the German Army was utterly beaten and its soldiers only too anxious to give themselves up. The next few days were spent in herding ever more prisoners to the rear.

The Battalion had reached Udine, when on the 2 May the Germans signed an instrument of unconditional surrender, adding another 230,000 prisoners to the many thousands already taken. The final total was nearly a million. For the second time Field-Marshal Alexander had fought a complete German Army to a standstill ending in complete surrender—first in North Africa and then in Italy. And in both campaigns the 3rd Battalion, as part of the 6th Armoured Division, had played a decisive part.

2nd Battalion: Germany—the Last Act

For the Guards Armoured Division the last act in Germany was played in two scenes. The first involved the advance from the Rhine to the Ems and beyond to Menslage. In the second the Division was switched from the Eastward advance of XXX Corps, and after a long drive of 100 miles they joined XII Corps in a northward thrust aimed at isolating Bremen and Hamburg.

Before the advance into the heart of Germany could take place, the Allied armies had to cross the formidable barrier of the Rhine which, on the sector facing 2nd British Army, was wide enough to demand an amphibious operation on some scale. On the night of 23 March the initial assault across the river took place, being supported at ten o'clock the next morning by the 6th British and 17th American Airborne Divisions. For two hours wave after wave of Dakotas spawned their parachutes, followed by Halifaxes towing and then releasing their giant gliders. It was the largest airborne operation of the war and completely successful. All objectives were captured, including five intact bridges over the next water obstacle, the River Issel.

At Rees, where the Guards Armoured Division were due to cross the Rhine, only six of the defenders, German Paratroops, allowed themselves to be taken alive. This desperate resistance rather slowed the expected timetable, but on the 28th the Division was put under orders to move, and two hours later were on their way. After a long and frustrating night drive, over chaotic roads, they reached the Calcar area on the near side of the river. They finally started to cross in the very early hours of the 30th, when it was still dark.

Almost as soon as the Division left the bridgehead, which had been secured by the 51st Highland Division, it became clear that they were not to be allowed a good gallop down the last straight. Their opponents for almost the rest of the way were to be from one or other of the German Parachute

Divisions. And one can only admire the skilful and determined opposition they put up for the remaining four weeks of the war. They had few resources, but these were employed with economy and resolution, and at no time could liberties be taken with these fanatical Nazis.

Nevertheless the Division advanced 100 miles in ten days. The lead was initially taken by 5th Guards Brigade, which reached Groenloe that night, in spite of a few sharp engagements on the way. 32nd Guards Brigade were not across the bridge until late on the 30th, but by the evening of the 31st, following a secondary route, they had reached Borculo. The next day the pattern was the same: a quick series of short advances punctuated by hard fought battles at squadron/company level. The two days were not unsuccessful, with 800 prisoners and much equipment being captured. In fact the number of prisoners was probably greater, since the highly efficient Dutch Resistance looked after a large number who did not pass through the Divisional cages.

By the evening of 1 April the Coldstream Group had cleared Enschede and early on the morning of the 2nd the Scots/Welsh Group attacked the airfield beyond. But the enemy had decamped during the night, and by ten in the morning the Battalions were on their way again. They were now in a slice of Holland which pushes itself into Germany, and they had a great welcome at Oldenzaal, where the advance was held up while the bridges were being repaired. As soon as one of them was ready No 2 Squadron (Major N. M. Daniel), with a company of Scots Guards, pushed on to Nordhorn. There all three bridges had been blown, but Daniel got his tanks across the crumbling masonry of one of them and took the town without trouble, while the remainder of both battalions concentrated west of the river.

It was now dark, but about 12 miles ahead lay the Ems River and just beyond it the Dortmund–Ems Canal. If the bridges at Lingen could be captured, one of the great barriers on the main road to Bremen would be lost to the enemy.

It was decided to try to capture the bridges that night.

Tanks do not usually operate in the dark, they are too blind. But the prize was considerable, and Lieutenant-Colonel Windsor Lewis got permission for the gamble. Daniel, already across, was to lead, with Right Flank Company, Scots Guards, mounted on all but his two leading troops of tanks. They were to be followed by No 3 and No 1 Squadrons, also with Scots Guardsmen aboard. No 3 Squadron (Major W. L. Consett) got safely across, but the already damaged bridge expired when No 1 tried to follow, leaving about half of both battalions and two indignant Commanding Officers on the wrong side. Major Consett took command of the advance of the two squadrons with their complement of Scotsmen.

The move started at 11.30, the night was dark and it was pouring with rain. Sergeant Townsend in the leading tank, and driving as fast as he dared, had little but the black ribbon of wet road to guide him. The move had plainly taken the enemy by surprise. A number of German soldiers and vehicles going quietly about their business were caught unawares and shot up. Return fire was wild and undisciplined until a well directed shot blew a track off Townsend's tank. At the time he was passing a German tank-transporter carrying a tank and a self-propelled gun. This blocked the road, and while Townsend destroyed both the transporter and its load, the troop commander, Lieutenant A. A. Upfill-Brown, found a way round through the fields and the advance continued. By three o'clock the Squadrons and the Scots Guards had reached the outskirts of Lingen on the west bank of the Ems.

By now the Germans had been thoroughly alerted, and a heavy if indiscriminate fire was opened on both tanks and Scotsmen. By the light of a blazing house one platoon of Scots Guards cleared the buildings on either side of the road, while two other platoons and the tanks made straight for the bridge. After a stiff fight the platoons got across, but as the leading tank tried to follow, the bridge went up. Undeterred, a second company stormed over in assault boats, but Lingen was too strongly held and without armoured support the bridgehead could not be maintained. The two companies were therefore ordered to withdraw while a deliberate assault was planned.

The attempt had only narrowly failed, but a valuable 12 miles had been made overnight. At first light the Household Cavalry discovered another bridge about three miles to the north of Lingen, which the Coldstream Group seized during the day. Lingen itself was not completely cleared until 5 April, when the Division was ordered to make for the River Weser, 80 miles away. A busy and complicated week of tough little actions followed, in which both Guards Brigades, on different routes, fought their way towards Bremen.

On 7 April the Scots/Welsh Group was put into the lead to take Lengerich. Right Flank and No 2 Squadron followed a rolling barrage, and at first it seemed that a quick result would be achieved. But resistance hardened and the two Battalion Commanders decided on a full-scale attack. This went in at three o'clock in the afternoon, following a rocket attack by RAF Typhoons and a heavy barrage from artillery and mortars. The defence crumbled, the town was occupied almost without trouble, and 60 Panzer Grenadiers were taken prisoner.

On the next day the Scots/Welsh Group rested, but that evening Major R. B. Hodgkinson, Second-in-Command of the Battalion, with Major H. Tweedie, his opposite number of the Scots Guards, were ambushed while looking for a harbour area for the night. All the party was killed, except for Major Hodgkinson. He was wounded and able to hide in a ditch until rescued later in the evening.

And so the advance continued, with one Regimental Group in each Brigade leading and the other trying to snatch a few hours respite for rest and maintenance, but all too often being called on to outflank a tough spot or to support the leading Group. The Scots/Welsh Group were in the lead again to Menslage, which was captured on the 10th. On 14 April the Division reached Capelln, where it was hoped that they would have a week to rest and refit. Although the fighting had not been as severe as in Normandy, or at Hechtel, casualties had not been light. Indeed the loss in tanks had been so considerable that the 2nd Battalion had to disband the Light Reconnaissance Squadron and redistribute its tanks among the other squadrons.

In the event, any programme of comprehensive and much needed maintenance had to be abandoned. The Division made the switch from XXX to XII Corps on 17 April, and that evening found the Scots/Welsh Group at Walsrode, ready to lead to Visselhovede the next day.

Reports that the Germans were reinforcing the area were soon confirmed. The next morning a two-squadron/company attack was needed to clear the village of Kettenburg, and a flanking movement showed that Ottingen was also strongly held. The outskirts of Visselhovede were not reached until that evening, too late to mount a fresh attack. The enemy consisted of German Marines, only recently sailors, and if they were not always skilled, they were brave, resourceful, well-led and disciplined. The attack on Visselhovede went in at dawn the next day, 19 April. The Coldstream Group, who had by-passed the town, attacked from the north, the Scots/Welsh Group from the south, and the place was soon cleared and occupied.

With the battle over everyone had settled down, rather too comfortably, to preparing dinners, when a well executed counter-attack by the German Marines fell on Group Headquarters. Bazooka shots set fire to tanks parked in the street, bullets from the garden whistled through the windows into the house, and Commanding Officers and Adjutants, signallers and clerks, suddenly found themselves fighting for their lives. Captain The Hon. N. H. C. Bruce, flat on the floor, tried to inform Brigade Headquarters of their predicament and gallantry, but the jump-lead to his tank was broken. Lieutenant-Colonel Windsor Lewis, and his adjutant Captain M. A. L. F. Pitt-Rivers, firing from the hip, kept up a brisk fire with their revolvers, holding the enemy at bay long enough for help to arrive.

It is the understandable, if insubordinate, wish of front line troops occasionally to witness the discomfiture of their superiors; but when the squadrons had stopped laughing they came to the aid of their beleaguered Headquarters. The first to arrive was Captain the Hon. A. B. Mildmay with No 3 Squadron, and he was rapidly followed by Lieutenant A. W. S. Wheatley with a troop from No 1. The fight that followed was a brisk one; many of the tanks fired off all their Besa machine gun ammunition and were reduced to taking pot-shots at individual Germans with their main guns. Gradually the squadrons got the upper hand, and 400 Marines, including their brigade commander, were rounded up. Eventually squadrons, companies and Group Headquarters could return to their interrupted dinners.

The next day 32nd Guards Brigade moved towards Rotenburg. To save casualties, and because the town contained a number of hospitals, it seemed worthwhile to try and get the garrison to surrender. Emissaries, including a German policeman previously captured by the Scots Guards, were sent in with a blood-curdling note about the town's fate if the surrender was refused. But no answer was received by the deadline, and an attack went in the following morning by both Coldstream and Scots/Welsh Groups. With minimal casualties to themselves (one killed and 20 wounded) they inflicted severe casualties on the enemy, and took so large a number of prisoners that no accurate record could be kept.

After Rotenburg came three days' rest at Sittensen, which the Scots/Welsh Group left on 26 April, moving through Zeven, which had already been taken by the Grenadiers and Coldstream. Their objective was the high ground eight miles East of Bremen, and a subsidiary objective of great importance was the prisoner of war camp at Westertimke, where some 8,000 Allied prisoners were held. During the day there was some heavy shelling and some fighting before they reached Ostertimke at nightfall. It was on that day that two emissaries, the Commandant and Paymaster of the Westertimke camp, arrived with an apparently generous offer, 'From the German Divisional Commander . . . to the Commander of the Guards Armoured Division', proposing a ten-hour truce during which the British prisoners of war would be handed over to the Guards Armoured Division. In fact the ten hours would have given the Germans just enough time to extricate themselves in good order. The offer was flatly refused.

On 27 April the Scots/Welsh Group first attacked Kirchtimke with No 1 and 2 Squadrons and two companies of Scots Guards. Their greatest difficulty lay in the mines with which the area had been liberally sown, and were causing the Sappers considerable trouble. At midday the reserve squadron, No 3, under Major C. A. LaT. Leatham, was ordered to go on and liberate the prisoners. His leading troop commander, Sergeant Glass, had his tank blown up on a mine. But No 3 Squadron went gingerly on. The risk was justified since no further mines were met.

At the far end of a wood were a number of huts, supposedly the quarters of the SS camp guards. No chances were taken, especially as an SP gun had been seen slipping away from an area marked as a hospital. Leatham's tanks set the huts ablaze; it was now pitch dark and the Scots Guards cleared them by the light of the flames. However the Germans had gone, and the village itself was also deserted, except for a few displaced Poles playing cards by the glare of the burning huts. Later that night No 13 Troop, under Lieutenant I. G. G. Davies, made contact with an outlying part of the camp. At dawn a Scots Guards patrol returned with the news that all was well at the main camp.

At nine o'clock in the morning Lieutenant-Colonel

Windsor Lewis and Major Leatham drove up to the camp. Of the 8,000 prisoners, about half were merchant seamen; of the soldiers, 42 were Guardsmen, mostly captured since the Rhine crossing. Two of these soldiers had been in enemy hands since Boulogne, one of whom had been in the Company that Lieutenant-Colonel Windsor Lewis had commanded there.

Postscript

For the second time in a generation, a long and bitter conflict had come to an end. In a short span of 30 years the Welsh Guards had spent nine years, nearly a third of their existence, at war. But as the firing died away and the battlefields of the world fell silent, new problems and tensions arose, not least between the Western Allies and Russia. It fell to the lot of the 3rd Battalion to be closely involved, almost at once, in one of the most difficult and distressing of these problems.

A month after the Armistice the 6th Armoured Division had advanced from the Adige into the Villach–Klagenfurt area of southern Austria, part of the British Occupation Zone. Battalion Headquarters was at Rosegg, 60 miles south of Judenburg, which marked the boundary of the British and Russian Occupation Zones.

Austria, like the rest of Europe at that time, was awash with uprooted peoples: individuals, groups, men, women, children, jobless mercenaries, private armies, and even small nations, all desperately on the move, seeking shelter, asylum or the barest means of staying alive somehow.

During the war the Germans had abducted from conquered territories some millions of people: Jews, Letts, Balts, Armenians, Azerbaijanies, Cossacks. Out of an unknown total, at least two million came from the Soviet Union and had been used as slave labour in German factories, on their farms, or on the construction of military installations. They had had no choice. Some, like the Cossacks who had never accepted the Soviet regime, were bitterly anti-communist and had greeted the Germans as liberators, had been recruited into military units and had fought against the Red Army or communist partisans in Yugoslavia. But whether they had co-operated willingly with the Germans or not, the Kremlin wanted them all back as traitors. Many did not relish the 're-education' in store for them and did not wish to return.

The political moves and counter-moves of the British and American governments were complicated, and their motives obscure. But both countries reached an agreement with the Russians that meant, in effect, that they would accede to the Russian demand and send all these people, willing or not, back to Russia, if necessary by force, and in some cases contrary to international law.

The political direction was adamant. In places as far apart as Egypt, Persia, France, Germany and even in England and the United States to which some of the Russians had been shipped, there were ugly and tragic scenes when the internees learned of their fate. In Europe, as stories began to trickle back, many soldiers became aware of the brutal end of those they had handed over, and found their task more and more distasteful. But the heroic resistance of the Red Army to the German invaders had made the Russians popular in the West; Allied propaganda had been at pains to portray Stalin in the benign guise of 'Uncle Joe', and the stories were slow of belief.

The situation which faced the 3rd Battalion, in the last week of May, was the return of part of the 15th Cossack Cavalry Corps, which was encamped about halfway between Klagenfurt and the grim reception committee of NKVD which awaited it at Judenburg. Just to the west, another large group of about 30,000 Cossacks were already, by force and deception, being handed over to the Russians amid scenes of the wildest despair. This group included not only units of traditional Cossack horsemen, but women, children, priests, schools and hospitals. The role of the cavalry had become less aggressive than simply protective of this miniature nation in its wanderings from the Russian steppes in search of a new homeland.

The 15th Cossacks were an efficient military organization, well disciplined and commanded by high-quality German officers, themselves cavalrymen. To their disappointment they had not been allowed to fight on the Eastern Front; Hitler had never quite trusted them, and although they had fought one successful battle against the Red Army towards the end of the war, they had for the most part been engaged against Tito's communist partisans.

They were first encountered by 6th Armoured Division early in May. A number of British officers had been impressed by their bearing at a review when, squadron by squadron, they swept past their commander, at full gallop, in perfect order. With their high fur hats, the jingle of their bits, their trumpeters on white horses, they added a touch of colour to the drab business of twentieth-century warfare.

On 26 May General Horatio Murray, commanding 6th Armoured Division, held a conference of his senior officers to discuss the handover to the Russians of those units of Cossacks which lay in his divisional area. The remainder of the Cossack Corps had been, or were to be, handed over by another division. At the conference General Murray made his distaste for the operation clear, just as in the previous weeks he had made it clear to all concerned that he would not try very hard to prevent any Cossack trying to escape. But he now had firm orders, which he was not prepared to flout openly. In spite of his sympathetic attitude it was not an easy conference. Discussion was long and sometimes heated. Lieutenant-Colonel Rose Price returned to his Battalion Headquarters that evening, where he issued his 'most ignoble instructions' to his company commanders. The Battalion's first task was to prepare a cage, at Weitensfeld, to which the Cossacks would be escorted by other units of the division, before being taken on to Judenburg. There were separate cages for officers and men. In the officers' compound, Rose Price met the senior Cossack officer, Major Ostrovsky, and confirmed to him that he, his officers and men, were indeed to be handed over to the Russians. It was in answer to a direct question, and neither he nor Major B. P. R. Goff the next day were prepared to lie or be party to what Corps Headquarters termed the 'use of deception'. Rose Price even allowed Ostrovsky to return down the long lines of horsemen as they moved towards the compound, inform his officers of the fact, and urge them to escape. As was intended, a few were able to do so. But by that evening most were in the cages.

The following morning, 28 May, the Cossack officers again demanded, this time of Goff, what their fate was to be. He also told them the truth. An immediate hubbub broke out, and what followed was almost as sickening for the Guardsmen as it was for the Cossacks, who absolutely refused to get on to the trucks waiting to take them to Judenberg. No threat of any kind of force, even shooting, would make them budge. By this time Colonel Rose Price had arrived. He ordered a flame-thrower to set fire to a neighbouring cornfield, a demonstration which shook the Cossacks. Rose Price followed this up with the threat that he would deliver them to the Russians—bound if necessary. The threat was reinforced by the appearance of a squad armed with clubs and telephone cable. A majority of the officers had already followed their priests into the waiting trucks. But a hard core of about 50 under Major Ostrovsky, remained obdurate, until one of them suggested that it would be better to go on the journey unbound; there might still be a chance of escape, or suicide, on the way. And indeed some of them had likely escape points suggested to them, with the assurance that their guards would fire carefully over their heads.

The convoy had not gone far when a British officer on a

motorcycle drew up beside the jeep in which Goff was personally escorting Ostrovsky. To Ostrovsky's surprise the jeep immediately turned and sped back to Weitensfeld. There they were greeted by cheerful and obviously relieved British officers. Ostrovsky and his group could be saved by signing the form which they waved at him; it certified that he was a White Russian emigré who had left the Soviet Union before 1938 and was not therefore liable to extradition. The others in the group, aided by a few leading questions, were not slow to catch on and sign the declaration. Eventually they were all to find themselves in a camp with several other White Russians, and in due course they were released to find homes and work in the West.

Although a lamentably large number of Cossacks were handed over, at least the number was substantially less than the NKVD had expected. The Russians sent a furious protest, but neither General Murray, the 6th Armoured Division, or the 3rd Battalion, Welsh Guards, minded at all.

Meanwhile, in northern Germany, the official end of the fighting produced what might have been a tricky situation when 32nd Guards Brigade was ordered to occupy the German naval base of Cuxhaven, its suburbs and the area round it. In addition to the 7,000 troops in Cuxhaven itself, the area swarmed with the German II Parachute Corps. Although the local surrender had been signed by the commander of the military area concerned, it was possible that the paratroopers, with their own fierce loyalties, might disobey. However all went well; the Scots/Welsh Group occupied the town and docks, while the Coldstream Group took the surrender of the parachute division. Some of them grumbled that, since they had not been defeated in battle (they had, of course, by Guards Armoured Division), they should not be treated as prisoners of war. But in the event their undoubted good discipline prevailed, and their own good staff-work in arranging their own surrender worked smoothly.

F

It was already known in the Division that sooner or later the armoured battalions would lose their tanks and revert to the infantry role. It was to be sooner than expected. On 19 May the 2nd Battalion moved to Rotenburg, and there, three weeks later, paraded for the last time in their tanks, and for the first time in four years as infantry once more.

On 19 June, a beautiful summer morning, the whole of Guards Armoured Division, tanks, guns, vehicles, all freshly painted, was drawn up on Rotenburg airfield for the Farewell to Armour parade. All the rank and fashion attended; at one moment there were no fewer than 14 Auster aircraft in the air at once, jostling to land and disgorge yet another general. Punctually at 11.30 Field-Marshal Sir Bernard Montgomery mounted the dais, and after taking the salute he inspected the Division. Then, to the strains of 'Auld Lang Syne' 250 tanks rolled past him, their guns dipping in salute, to disappear in a cloud of dust over a slight rise half a mile away. After a short pause the dismounted crews marched back past him to the music of the massed bands. The Field-Marshal then addressed the Division, saying in part, 'In the sphere of armoured warfare, you have set a standard that will be difficult for those that come after to reach . . . now you are to return to your traditional role of infantry. Some of you may wonder why this is so. Firstly, the King wishes it. Secondly, the Brigade of Guards as a whole is anxious that this should be done. Thirdly, I myself, an Infantry soldier of many years service, would say to you that you are needed as Infantry.' Finally all ranks were moved by the sincere tribute he paid to their commander, General Allan Adair: 'He never failed me, and he never failed you.' The parade, and the Field-Marshal's words, were an emotional climax to the years of waiting and training, hard fighting, and final victory.

Before closing the account of the war years, it is proper to pay tribute to those who backed the battalions so staunchly in battle—those who in histories, long or short, seldom get the limelight, but without whose unsung support, the courage and sacrifice of the rifle companies and fighting squadrons would be in vain. Within the battalions, the Padre, the Medical Officers, the Quartermasters and their staffs are vital. Stretcher-bearers, cooks, drivers, signallers, despatch-riders and clerks, all have an essential, difficult, and often dangerous part to play. Closely supporting the battalions are gunners, Sappers and supply columns of the Royal Army Service Corps, to name but a few. No Welsh Guardsman who fought in the Second World War would like this account to close without special mention of the Leicestershire Yeomanry, the Lothian and Border Horse, the Ayrshire Yeomanry, or the Light Aid Detachment from REME, which gave such unstinted backing to the 2nd Battalion. And the 1st and 3rd Battalions owe a particular debt of gratitude to their brother Guardsmen, X Company Scots Guards, who fought so long and gallantly with the 1st Battalion, and the company of Grenadiers who fought as part of the 3rd Battalion in Italy.

At home, there were the Guards Depot at Caterham, the Training Battalion at Esher, and the Armoured Training Wing at Pirbright, turning civilians into soldiers tough enough and professional enough to take their place in the battle-hardened battalions. And last, but by no means least, mention must be made of the Welsh Guards Families Association, run so ably and sympathetically by Lady Stanier. By relieving the anxiety of the Guardsman abroad over any problem his family might have at home, it did much to contribute to the success of the battalions in the field.

7 THE POST-WAR YEARS

The First Ten Years: 1945–55

During Queen Victoria's reign of 63 years, the heyday of Empire, the British Army took part in at least 230 major or minor wars, expeditions, skirmishes, actions of one sort or another in all corners of the world. Kipling called them the 'Savage Wars of Peace'. Following the upheaval of the Second World War, the dissolution of Empire proved no less strenuous. And equally far flung. Since 1945 the Regiment, or detachments of it, have served in 16 different countries, and in some of them two or three times.

After the war demobilization and disbandment started fairly soon. The 3rd Battalion was the first to go. By the autumn of 1945 they had returned from Italy, and after leave were posted to Hawick, and later to Amersham, where they were disbanded in April 1946. As a wartime battalion this was to be expected. But the loss of the 2nd Battalion which, although it had only been raised in 1939, was a regular battalion, came as a shock. They had continued to serve in Germany, near Cologne, until March 1947, when they returned to Caterham. On 16 June their colours, now in the Guards Chapel, were returned to the King at Windsor Castle, and on 1 July the Battalion was placed in suspended animation.

Meanwhile the 1st Battalion, soon to stand as the only battalion in the Regiment, had sailed for Palestine in

October 1945, under command of Lieutenant-Colonel R. B. Hodgkinson. It was a strong battalion, having been made up with drafts from both the 2nd and 3rd Battalions, and although most of the Guardsmen had yet to see service outside England, many of the officers, Warrant Officers and NCOs were experienced.

After the hardships of war in Europe, and the restrictions of rationing at home, they looked forward to an enjoyable, if busy, tour in a pleasant climate. And for the first winter, peace-time soldiering came up to expectations. Duties were light, training varied, and there was plenty of sport. Even oranges and grapefruit seemed exotic after the dull fare of rationed England.

But it was not to last. As winter warmed to spring, and spring blazed into summer, so the political situation simmered and finally boiled over. The reasons were ancient and complex. In brief, in 1917 the British government, as a gesture to rally the sympathy of world Jewry behind the Allied cause, committed themselves to the establishment of a national home for Jews in Palestine. Modern Palestine included the Old Testament kingdom of Judea, which had lasted on and through Roman times. But the Arabs, who had become the majority during the long hegemony of the Ottoman Empire, regarded any influx of Jews as a threat to their soil and livelihood. Trouble flared in the 1930s, lay dormant during the war, and flared again, more violently, in 1946. Now many thousands of European Jews, homeless and desperate survivors of Hitler's brutal policy of extinction, took up the commitment to a national home with increasing pressure. Legally, and illegally, they flooded into what they regarded as their historic homeland, a country which the Arabs, with equal passion, also regarded as home by right of settlement over 1,000 years. The pattern was set for a situation with which the British Army was to become only too familiar in years to come: keeping the peace between rival groups separated by race, politics, religion, or all three.

The Post-war Years

During the next two years, with little let-up, the Battalion was engaged in the always monotonous, usually tiring, and sometimes dangerous routine of trying to preserve law and order. There were cordon and search operations, road blocks had to be established, roads, often mined, to be patrolled, and endless railway guards to be provided. At one time or another their activities covered most of the country, from Dan to Beersheba. In two years they moved their base camp no less than five times in the attempt to cope with the ever widening requirement, usual in this type of operation, of too few troops chasing too much trouble.

In April 1947 the problem was referred to the United Nations, and in November of that year the partition of Palestine, between Jews and Arabs was approved. But calls on the Battalion did not cease; rather the reverse: both sides were now taking up positions for the war which they knew must follow the British withdrawal.

It was with some relief that on 28 March 1948 the Welsh Guards embarked for home. On the way to Haifa the convoy was halted by a brisk engagement in which the Arabs were attacking a Jewish settlement. With little desire to intervene, the Guardsmen debussed, watched the battle, and when it was all over continued placidly down to the docks and embarked for home.

In April the Battalion assembled in Chelsea Barracks for their first round of public duties since the war, and duly mounted King's Guard on 9 June, after a gap of ten years. It was during this tour at Chelsea that Home Service Clothing was reissued (pyjamas were issued to the soldiers for the first time), and that London ceremonial again took on its prewar plumage. The first great occasion on which the Welsh Guards paraded in Guard Order was on 25 May, when the King presented the 1st Battalion with new Colours in the gardens of Buckingham Palace. For the older Comrades the occasion was a nostalgic reminder of the past, and for some of the younger ones a first glimpse of part of the tradition which had sustained them through the years of the war.

The new Colours were subsequently trooped on the Birthday Parade in June, when the Battalion found both the Escort and No 2 Guard. The parade was commanded by Lieutenant-Colonel A. W. A. Malcolm, whose prewar eye for ceremonial detail was of inestimable value after a decade of battle dress. The old Colours were laid up in St David's Cathedral the following year.

In the spring of 1950 the Battalion left for its fi st tour in post-war Germany, under command of Lieutenant-Colonel D. G. Davies-Scourfield. The Battalion was stationed at Wuppertal, as part of 4th Guards Brigade, with whom they were to serve three times in Germany over the next 20 years. The primary role of British and American forces in Germany had changed. They were no longer armies of occupation in a defeated country, but a garrison against any westward adventure by their former ally, Russia.

After two years at Chelsea it was now for the Battalion to prove that they were as professional in the field as they were immaculate on the parade-ground—battle dress and scarlet, the warp and woof of a Guardsman's life. Drill standards were kept up, and the Birthday Parade carried out each year at Dusseldorf. But the priority was training, for which excellent facilities were available at Sennelager and Putlos. And it was at Wuppertal that the Welsh Guards were visited, for the last time, by their old Colonel, the Duke of Windsor, who still showed a perennial interest in all their activities. He was obviously moved when the Sergeants Mess rose and sang 'God Bless the Prince of Wales'.

In March 1952 the Battalion moved nearer to the focus of the cold war—Berlin. In 1948 the Russians had tried to blockade the western sector, not only the British, American and French garrisons, but the inhabitants as well. For 323 days all supplies, even fuel for heating, had to be flown in. (In 1961 the Russians would again make a nuisance of themselves when, overnight on 13 August, they erected the wire and concrete of the Berlin Wall, knifing the city in two.) But if the political climate was frosty, Berliners were warm and welcoming and the lights on the Kufurstendam were bright. A little training could be carried out in the Grunewald, and the Spandau Prison Guard, mounted in rotation with guards from the American, French and Russian armies over seven top Nazi war criminals, kept an edge on drill and turnout.

After celebrating the St David's Day of 1953 in Berlin, the 1st Battalion, now under command of Lieutenant-Colonel A. C. W. Noel, returned to England for six months before going to Egypt. Their task during this short period, when they were stationed at Aldershot and then Windsor, was to prepare for, and take part in, the Coronation of Her Majesty, Queen Elizabeth II. All regiments of Foot Guards provided a marching contingent and a detachment of street-liners. It was an exhausting day in which no one was on their feet for less than 12 hours. The weather was less than kind, providing enough rain to soak the bearskins; an officer who weighed his on return to barracks found that it tipped the scales at ten pounds. No wonder there were some stiff necks that night. But nothing could spoil that day. It was an occasion which no one would have missed: from early morning, when the news of Sir Edmund Hillary's conquest of Everest hummed through the waiting crowds, through the passing of the processions, alive with music and colour which, splendid though they were, were no more than an adequate setting for the great jewel of the Coronation coach itself, bearing the crowned Queen and the Duke of Edinburgh back to Buckingham Palace.

After the Coronation the Battalion settled at Windsor, where there were duties at the castle, and from where they sallied on a series of recruiting marches in Wales. On 9 July the Welsh Guards were much honoured to hear that the Queen had appointed the Duke of Edinburgh as Colonel of the Regiment, in place of the Earl of Gowrie, who had won his Victoria Cross at the Battle of Omdurman, and who had retired owing to ill health. His Royal Highness paid his first visit to the 1st Battalion in October, on the eve of its departure to Egypt on the *Empire Ken*.

The *Empire Ken* docked at Port Said on 13 October, where the Battalion was met by Commanding Officers of each of the other Regiments of Foot Guards. With the arrival of the Welsh Guards, the Canal Zone had drawn a full house. Egypt had not been immune from the rising tide of nationalism in the Middle East. And the Anglo-Egyptian Treaty of 1936, which gave the British certain rights, could, by those with an interest to do so, easily be represented as an example of oppressive colonialism. None of the political parties in Egypt, therefore, could afford to show moderation in the re-negotiating of the Treaty which was now due. By the time the Battalion arrived the worst of the troubles, arson and rioting in Cairo, were over. But tensions remained high until a new Treaty was signed in October 1954, under which the British agreed to withdraw all their troops from Egypt. There were guard duties to be performed on the enormous dumps of stores and ammunition, on the railway, on the El Firdan Bridge and on married quarters.

The Battalion settled first into a miserable camp on the canal-side at El Ballah, but which with ingenuity and hard work was made habitable. Later they moved into good, brick-built barracks at Moascar. In spite of security duties, some training in the desert was achieved, the Queen's Birthday was marked by the proper parade, there was time for sport and leave, and a holiday camp was set up on the shores of the Red Sea which provided bathing, goggle fishing and relaxation. For the more enterprising there was the trip through the desert and mountains of Sinai to St Catherine's Monastery, where the traveller was greeted by Brother Gabriel, who wore German army boots under his cassock, and who had an unquenchable thirst for gin. But the Canal Zone was a claustrophobic place for soldiering, and

Support Company deemed themselves lucky to be sent to
Aqaba, in Transjordan, for a couple of months over
Christmas 1955.

A New Epoch: 1956–65

In March 1956 the Battalion, under the command of
Lieutenant-Colonel C. A. LaT. Leatham, returned to
England. After five months at Shornecliff it moved to Chelsea,
still a grimy old Victorian pile, but which by their next
occupation would have been swept away and replaced by the
clean, modern lines of the present building. Sixteen months
later they moved to Pirbright, where they remained until
December 1960, when they left for their second tour in
Germany.

There is never a single date to identify the end of one
epoch and the start of another. But the next few years, first
at home and then in Germany, showed a marked change in
the concepts and attitudes of the British Army, in the
conditions of service, in weapons and equipment, and
therefore in tactics. After the economy of the immediate
post-war years, new, open and comfortable barracks, but with
more privacy for the soldier, replaced the walled, prison-like
structures of the nineteenth century. More important,
modern and convenient married quarters were being provided for families. Catering improved out of all recognition,
and if the Services tend to fall behind in the pay race from
time to time, by and large the pay and allowances of all ranks
became much more in line with their civilian counterparts
than had been the case before.

The first two years after the Battalion's return from
Egypt were, for the most part, occupied by public duties
from Chelsea or Pirbright, punctuated by various special
occasions. On St David's Day 1957 the leeks were presented
by HM Queen Elizabeth the Queen Mother with her
invariable grace and humour. On 27 April HRH the Colonel,

with a detachment of the Regiment, accepted from the Lord Mayor of Cardiff the illuminated scroll which recorded that the honour of the Freedom of the City of Cardiff had been conferred on the Welsh Guards. This honour had already been granted by Swansea in 1948 and Aberystwyth in 1953; Caernarvon was to follow in 1958. The history of granting freedoms is an ancient one, evolving from an Act of 1327 which exempted the Mayor and Commonalty of London from compulsory military service outside the city boundaries, and which thus established the right to prevent the entry of 'The Sovereign's Troop' into the city. But over the years, if the City desired to show special confidence in or approbation of a particular regiment, they extended to it the grant of Freedom, usually expressed as 'the right to march through the streets with drums beating, colours flying and bayonets fixed'. The Local Government Act of 1933 allowed other cities to grant this privilege. But even when granted, the regiment so honoured must still obtain the mayor's permission before the right can be exercised.

In June of 1958 the Regiment also found the Guard of Honour at the Empire Games, when it was announced to cheering crowds that Prince Charles had been created Prince of Wales.

From 1958 to 1960 the Battalion concentrated on some fairly hard training, and in June 1958 they sent a composite company to Cyprus to reinforce the 1st Battalion, Irish Guards, who had been hurried there to deal with the heightened tension between the Greek and Turkish communities.

The first straw in the wind of new weapons and tactics was the issue of the SLR rifle in February 1959; it required a new arms drill which abolished the 'slope'. In 1959 the Welsh Guards were attached to 16th Independent Parachute Brigade, to carry out Mobility Trials with light scales of equipment and deployment by air. Three considerable exercises followed. The first, in Beverly aircraft to Northern

Ireland, took place in August 1959. The second, after a rough trip in destroyers of the Royal Navy, was a winter exercise for part of the Battalion in Norway. And the third, again by air, was a desert exercise with 1st Guards Brigade in Libya. More than anything else these swift transitions from snow to sand and back to the gravel of the parade ground indicated the evolving pattern of army life. But perhaps, after all, a date can be given which marked the change from an older to a newer epoch. In November 1960 the Battalion moved to Germany, and for the last time they trooped by sea. Thereafter, in humdrum fashion, they would depart by air. The traditional troopship, steaming slowly away from the quayside to the strains of 'Auld Lang Syne' from the Regimental Band, had gone for ever.

After their arrival at Hubbelrath the Battalion found that the pace had, if anything, quickened. The yearly cycle of training in Germany, at Sennelager, Putlos and Vogelsang, took place, and in the summer of 1961 the Battalion trained for six weeks at Leopoldsburg, in Belgium, where the Irish Guards had had as bitter a fight in 1944 as the Welsh battling at Hechtel. The dead of both Regiments lie in the cemetery at Leopoldsburg; and a visit to Hechtel, led by the Commanding Officer, Lieutenant-Colonel V. G. Wallace, who had fought there, showed that the local inhabitants had not forgotten their liberators.

In addition to the normal BAOR training the Battalion was selected as the British contingent in the Mobile Land Force. This was a representative NATO force designed to go at short notice to either of the vulnerable NATO flanks, north to Norway or east to Greece. In addition to the obvious military role of providing quick reinforcement to these sparsely defended extremities of NATO, there was also a political objective. By making this force an international one, the intention was to show that all NATO countries were committed against a quick Russian grab against the weaker countries of the alliance.

The first MLF exercise in 1961 was a minor affair in which a small detachment from each of the participating countries was air-lifted to Sardinia. The next, in October 1962, was more ambitious. The Welsh Guards, together with American, Belgian and German battalions and supporting arms, were flown to Greece. The Battalion landed at Larissa, in pouring rain, on a near flooded airfield, and found themselves overnight in a completely flooded staging camp. The transport provided by the Greek army consisted of well used American $2\frac{1}{2}$-tonners, relics of the war. In spite of this the Battalion managed to arrive to the minute in their assembly area 120 miles away—the only unit to do so. They then took up a defensive position in the hills northeast of Salonica, overlooking the River Strimon, one of the historic gateways into Greece for an invader from the north. The following summer there was a signals exercise well into the Arctic Circle in Norway; it amused the second-in-command to delay a reconnaissance of the Russian border for the pleasure of making it, in broad daylight, at two o'clock in the morning.

After the Birthday Parade at Dusseldorf there was more training at Sennelager, and again at Soltau. In August Lieutenant-Colonel P. R. Leuchars took over command of the Battalion in time to take it to Larzac in the South of France, up in the hills behind the Mediterranean. Even then training for the year had not quite finished. Hardly had the Battalion returned from the warmth of the South of France than they left for a final, cold and wet exercise on the Baltic.

After this last exercise the Welsh Guards, as well trained a peacetime battalion as has ever been, returned to the newly-built Chelsea Barracks, where they were to remain for 18 months. But their travels were still not quite over. In June 1964 they flew to Canada for six weeks training in Alberta. Their Canadian hosts were as generous as they were helpful, and it was at once chastening and inspiring to Household troops, with their tendency to self-satisfaction, to

161

discover that the Canadian regiments with whom they worked boasted as fierce a loyalty to the Crown as themselves, and were equally efficient.

1965 was a memorable year. The Regiment celebrated its fiftieth anniversary; on St David's Day the salute was taken by Major-General Fox-Pitt, who had served with the Regiment, as an Ensign, from the first. And to make a family occasion complete, the leeks were presented by Mrs Stevenson, the widow of the Regiment's first and most respected Regimental Sergeant-Major. How proud he would have been.

Also in that year Sir Winston Churchill, the great wartime Prime Minister, died. No one who saw, or took part in, the State Funeral will forget the solemn procession winding its way through the streets of London, from Westminster Hall to St Paul's Cathedral, to the insistent thud of muffled drums, the minor strains of the 'Dead March In Saul', and the heart-rendering cry of the pipes breaking into the 'Flowers of the Forest'.

In May, when new Colours were again presented to the 1st Battalion by Her Majesty the Queen, it seemed impossible that almost a quarter of a century had passed since her father, King George VI, had granted the same honour, at a similar ceremony, also in the gardens of Buckingham Palace. The following month the new Colours were again trooped on the Birthday Parade, commanded by the Regimental Lieutenant-Colonel, Colonel M. C. Thursby-Pelham, when, for the first time, the Queen wore the uniform of the Regiment. Later in the month the old Colours were laid up in the Guards Chapel by His Royal Highness, the Colonel.

The Savage Wars of Peace: 1965-76

In September 1965 the Battalion was posted to Aden, under command of Lieutenant-Colonel P. J. N. Ward, later to become the first Welsh Guardsman to be the Major-General commanding the Household Division. Aden was one of the first acquisitions of Great Britain's Victorian Empire. In 1839 a Captain Haines of the Indian Navy landed, with 700 soldiers, to exact compensation from the Sultan of Lahej for the alleged maltreatment of the crew of a British ship wrecked there two years before. Haines persuaded the Sultan to cede the Aden peninsula to the British government in return for an annual pension of 6,000 dollars. Aden became a Dependency of the Government of India and so remained until it became a Crown Colony in 1937. With the advent of steam it had become a vital link, as a coaling station, on the route to India.

Great Britain's support of a Jewish home in Palestine, coupled with the abortive Suez campaign of 1956, had done nothing to enhance her prestige in the Middle East. The rising tide of Arab nationalism, supported by Egypt, bedevilled by an old claim of the Yemen to the Aden Territories, and with Russia vigorously stirring the pot, was not to be denied. Britain was prepared to hand over power to a responsible government, but as usual the British soldier found himself trying to keep the peace between local contenders for eventual office. In this case the conflicting interest was between the National Liberation Front, which represented the up-country tribes and the Yemen, and the cosily initialled Front for the Liberation of South Yemen, FLOSY, which represented the townspeople of Aden and the Aden TUC. They briefly joined forces, but split again. In 1963 a State of Emergency had been declared and the Battalion arrived to find this internecine rivalry being pursued with enthusiasm.

The Battalion was quartered in Little Aden, where, under command of 24th Infantry Brigade, they found themselves engaged in the internal security duties familiar to the situation. Quite soon afterwards they were involved in the high, hot, arid Radfan, the home of the fiercely independent

163

Quteibi tribesmen, who for centuries had exercised the right of exacting toll on merchants, and pilgrims to Mecca, along the caravan route from Aden which winds for 80 miles to Dhala, 6,000 feet up in their inhospitable country. The imposition of law and order was against all tribal instincts: mercantile brigandage, vendetta, and the sheer fun of guerrilla warfare. Unlike the urban terrorists in Aden itself, their motives were not primarily political. Backed by Egyptian gold, the opportunities for capable and self-respecting mercenaries were too good to miss. In 1963 they cut the Aden–Dhala road. Thereafter a British battalion was stationed at Habilayn, where a basic camp, together with an air-strip, was constructed, from which it was possible to give administrative and air support to operations in this desolate area. It was a fragmented form of warfare. Not only the Battalion, but companies and even platoons were split up in what became very much a junior leaders campaign.

On 16 March a section of Prince of Wales Company on Picquet Hill was attacked by small arms fire and by blindicide rockets. Both of the section's non-commissioned officers were wounded. But Guardsman H. Holland from Llangefni took command and drove off the attack. His initiative and courage were recognized by the award of the Military Medal. On another occasion, by dragging their coats No 2 Company nicely fooled the tribesmen who blundered into a carefully laid trap; three of them were killed and six wounded. 59 Sergeant Edwards handled his platoon with such skill that he too was awarded the Military Medal. In November 1966, after further internal security duties, the Battalion returned home to Windsor.

During the next two years the Regiment strengthened their bonds with Wales by a number of visits, and twice took part in the Cardiff Searchlight Tattoo, the annual and major military event in the Principality. In May 1968 they also took part in a unique parade in which all regiments of Foot Guards together received the Freedom of the Royal Borough of Windsor. Each regiment provided a colour party and a large marching contingent, and it is one of the very few occasions when every regiment of Foot Guards has received the Queen in line.

But as usual those years provided training and travel as well as ceremony. In June 1968 a rifle company trained with the 2nd Battalion, Scots Guards, in Germany. In August a platoon joined the 1st Battalion, Grenadier Guards, in Sharjah for nine months. In the autumn of 1968 the whole Battalion, now under command of Lieutenant-Colonel N. Webb-Bowen, had a short spell in Cyprus, to garrison the Sovereign Base Area of Dhekelia. Routine guard duties took up a certain amount of time, but Cyprus was comparatively peaceful, and opportunities for training and recreation were not neglected.

On its return to England the Battalion moved to Pirbright. From there it took part in the rare ceremony of the Investiture of the Prince of Wales at Caernarvon Castle.

After his defeat of Llywelyn ap Gruffydd in 1282, Edward I took up residence in Caernarvon and started to build the great castle whose majestic ruins still dominate the town. He was anxious to pacify the Welsh, and in 1301 he created and presented his son, 'that was born in Wales and could never speak a word of English', to the Welsh people, as Prince of Wales and Earl of Chester. The next Prince of Wales, Edward the Black Prince, was created in 1343, and formally invested with Coronet, gold ring and silver rod. He was also made Duke of Cornwall. Since then the eldest son of the sovereign is by birth Duke of Cornwall, and with a few exceptions Prince of Wales by creation at the pleasure of the sovereign.

The creation and investiture are separate, and it was not until this century that the investiture as we know it today has taken place in Wales. Either it had taken place at Westminster, or the Prince was simply introduced as such to the House of Lords following the issue of Letters Patent. In

1911 Mr Lloyd George suggested that the then Prince of Wales, the future Edward VIII, the first Colonel of the Welsh Guards, be formally invested at Caernarvon.

On 1 July 1969, Prince Charles (soon to be Colonel of Welsh Guards), was invested as Prince of Wales. After the reading of the Letters Patent, in English and Welsh, the Prince paid homage to the Queen with the words 'I, Charles, Prince of Wales, do become your liege man of life and limb and earthly worship, and faith and truth I will bear unto you to live and die against all manner of folks.' The culmination of the ritual was when the Prince was presented to the people of Wales by the sovereign, first at Queen Eleanor's Gate, then at the King's Gate and lastly in the lower ward of the Castle. Only at that moment did he become the ruling prince of the people and country of Wales.

In September the Battalion went to Norway to train with the Norwegian Brigade North. By happy coincidence this formation was commanded by Colonel Ivar Froystadt, who had won an MC while fighting with the 2nd Battalion in 1944/5. He gave the Welsh Guards a tremendous welcome, and between exercises his hospitality was much appreciated.

In late October a strong company went to Fort Hood in Texas, in an exchange with a company from 1st US Armoured Division who came to Pirbright. The exchange was a great success: Guardsmen always seem to get on with the American Army.

In March 1970 the 1st Battalion, under the command of Lieutenant-Colonel J. W. T. Malcolm, again found themselves in Germany, under command of 4th Guards Armoured Brigade. Their immediate problem was to learn how to handle 90 Armoured Personnel Carriers. Not since 1941, when the 2nd Battalion took to tanks, had Welsh Guardsmen been faced by so technical a challenge. But always adaptable they soon mastered their new role as mechanized infantry, and learned to think and move at 30 mph instead of the traditional three.

During that winter the Battalion was warned for service in Belfast. APCs were put away while they learned the techniques required for dealing with troubled areas of the Falls and Shankhill Road. But the tour was postponed, cancelled, and in the way of the Army almost immediately reimposed. A week later the Battalion's rugger team, as holders, were playing in the final of the Army Cup at Aldershot. A tense game had gone into extra time, and just as Guardsman W. Williams (66) was preparing to kick the winning penalty goal, the Commanding Officer was tapped on the shoulder and told, 'You move to Belfast the day after tomorrow.' Goal and move were achieved with precision.

One day, when passions may mercifully have cooled, a future historian will be able to tell in full the story, still unfinished, of the British Army in Northern Ireland. Meanwhile only a bare account of the Welsh Guards' involvement, typical of so many other regiments, can be given.

During their first tour the Battalion was quartered in a factory in the northern suburbs of Belfast, except for No 2 Company who were attached to the Parachute Regiment at Andersonstown. The Battalion had no specific area of responsibility, but operated a sort of 'Rent-a-Company' system in response to the many calls for reinforcement in support of over-stretched police or army. It was frustrating and disheartening work, but a lot of lessons were learned which would stand in good stead in future tours; in particular, the Battalion's speed of reaction when called for became notable.

The Battalion was in fact back in Belfast after only nine months. Meanwhile they returned to Germany, where there was leave and plenty of sport, including skiing, to be enjoyed. There was also a visit by the Colonel, the Duke of Edinburgh, who stayed with them for four days.

When the Battalion returned to Ulster they faced an even tougher situation than the one they had left. Bombing or shooting incidents in central Belfast took place almost

167

nightly; and in some parts of the city the IRA had established such control that these became 'No-Go' areas into which police and army seldom penetrated. Clearly more positive measures were required. In the first, operation Segment, a major part of the centre of the city was sealed off, so successfully that it was several months before a bomb was exploded in the restricted area, and once again citizens could go about their daily business in a more normal way.

On 21 July the IRA countered by placing 22 bombs round the boundaries of the Segment area, one of which killed Sergeant P. Price (06), Driver Cooper of the RCT and nine civilians. That night the IRA attacked a Welsh Guards patrol, with a claimed loss of six gunmen. The following day the Battalion had information that there was a bomb factory in the Markets. A cordon and search operation was completely successful. A large haul of explosives was found, and a senior IRA man was captured in his birthday suit—streaking.

At the end of July 1972, under Lieutenant-Colonel M. R. Lee, the Battalion took part in Operation Motorman, which was designed to re-establish both army and police in the 'No-Go' areas and to ensure that Government writ was reimposed in these IRA feifdoms. The operation was a success, and the Battalion returned to Munster with added laurels.

At the end of 1972 the Battalion moved from Germany to Chelsea Barracks, from which, a year later, they carried out their third tour in Ulster. Meanwhile in 1973 the rugger team won the Army Cup for the third time in four years. In June of that year they provided a particularly impressive Escort to the Colour on a Birthday Parade which was commanded by Colonel Malcolm, as his father had commanded it 24 years before.

When in November the Welsh Guards returned to Ulster for four months, they were stationed in the rural area of South Armagh, less two companies which again did duty in Belfast. Unfortunately Guardsman Roberts was killed by a landmine within a week of arrival. This was their only casualty during the tour. Indeed so good were the Battalion's discipline and professional approach, that incidents of any kind were minimal. Even so, the dangers and strain of Northern Ireland took their toll, falling particularly hardly on young wives, who had to stay at home to face, alone, the daily insistence of television and newspapers on the violence in Ulster. Recruiting, as with the rest of the Army, fell off, and a number of soldiers left.

The Battalion returned to Chelsea in March 1974, and between October and December Prince of Wales and No 2 Company each spent separate six-week tours in Sharjah on the Persian Gulf. In December Lieutenant-Colonel P. R. G. Williams took over from Lieutenant-Colonel M. R. Lee, and the Battalion left for Caterham, in time to celebrate, in 1975, the St David's Day which marked the Regiment's 60th anniversary. It also gave the whole Regiment, past and present, the opportunity to greet HRH the Prince of Wales as its new Colonel. He followed his father, the Duke of Edinburgh, who earlier in the month had become Colonel of the Grenadiers, who for 22 years was the Regiment's longest serving Colonel, and who had exercised such a deep personal interest and influence in all its affairs.

The Regiment's 60th year was marred by an event which took place on 27 August, when the IRA planted a bomb in the Caterham Arms. It exploded at 9.31 when the pub was full, not only with civilians but a number of Guardsmen. Several civilians were wounded, also 20 of the Guardsmen, some very severely. Guardsman Thomas lost both legs and one arm, Lance-Sergeant Ollerhed a leg, and Guardsman G. Watkins also lost a leg. As soon as they were fit to be visited, the new Colonel came to the hospital where the wounded Guardsmen were lying. Public response was also immediate and practical, producing a substantial sum for the Regimental Comforts Fund.

Starting in October the Welsh Guards spent six months

abroad, again in Cyprus, this time wearing the blue beret of the United Nations Force in Cyprus, to exercise yet again the mixture of tact, firmness and professional skill which no other army in the world can bring to the duties of preserving peace in an explosive racial or political situation.

On Friday, 30 July 1976, there took place an event which must be unique in the history of any regiment in the British Army. On that day the more seriously wounded in the Caterham explosion made a pilgrimage to the summit of Snowdon. Partly by the mountain train, and partly by the Royal helicopter, these men, led by their Colonel, made their way to the summit. Guardsman Thomas, with three false limbs, achieved the last 200 yards unaided.

The Welsh Guards have had their adventures since; they have served in Berlin and yet again in Northern Ireland. But let the future historian take up the tale from that moment, when the Prince of Wales stood with a number of his bitterly wounded but undaunted Guardsmen, on the highest point of his Principality.

INDEX

Index

Index

Index